The Role Of Leadership In Change Management

How To Use Continuous Innovation To Create Radically Successful Businesses, How to Change Your Mind, And How To Change Things When Change is Hard

By: DR. Felicity Gray

Contents

Introduction

They say that there are only two constants in life: Death and Taxes. In addition, if the Grim Reaper were to work in the IRS, they would be the same thing altogether.

However, one other constant element governs everything in life: its name is Change.

Change is one inherent force that drives everything to enter into a new state of being, for better or worse. Change is the reason why lifeforms rise and fall. It is the reason why civilizations and empires are founded and, for the same reason, are ended.

In the field of business, Change is what drives innovation. It is the sole reason why the industries and technologies that we see and enjoy now came into being in the first place. In addition, more so, it is sparked by the breakthroughs and successes of others.

If, for example, the Wright Brothers failed at their little stunt of an experiment in Kitty Hawk, then all of us would still by flying in blimps across the world now, or not at all.

However, here is the problem: Change is a double-edged sword. In as much as it pushes things forward, it can also push others to the side. When the mobile phone was introduced in the late 90s, landline telephone companies scoffed at this seeming novelty of a device. Surely, this hand held blocky abomination would never dethrone the landline phone.

Yet here we are, 2 decades later, doing all of our personal and business communications through pocket devices. The telephone might not have become obsolete but it is definitely dethroned as the go-to telecomm device for people. Many children born in recent years do not even know what a telephone looks like.

The point is that Change always happens, whether you like it or not. For businesses, the goal then is this: Adapt or Die.

However, change is not something that is easy to embrace. For a business to succeed in changing, change must be embraced from the top and must permeate through every level and department. This is where leaders come into play as the performance of companies are utterly dependent on how they themselves make decisions that ultimately affect their employees, stakeholders, and other leaders.

A management style that is focused and optimized for change, then, would be the best route to take. This would be necessary especially in recent years when change is all the more rampant across all markets and sectors of society.

In addition, with all things, adopting change management into one's leadership style takes time and practice. This also requires one to learn the basics of the concept. In addition, when one fully understands this management style, there is then the challenge of applying it at every level of the business and handling the potential fallout that could arise from such changes.

If your intention is to make your business as responsive to change as possible and take the next step forward, now it is time to prepare yourself as we delve into the style of Managed geared in response to, and in anticipation of, Change.

Chapter I: The Role of Change in Business

First, one question needs to be asked:

Why is Change Important for Organizations?

Why do businesses need to even acknowledge the fact that change is the one constant element that they must never, ever underestimate? The short answer is that change is what drives sectors, especially the ones that the business relies on for survival, ever forward.

Change is important in business because it is what motivates companies to maintain a competitive edge over the others. Those that fail or outright refuse to change are what we called "dinosaurs": large, bloated entities that are out of touch with society and whose unwillingness to adapt to current trends would eventually lead to their fading into obscurity.
In addition, in almost all epochs, change in the market is often manifested in three ways. These are:

1. Technology

Efficiency has always been an issue for businesses. Back then, it was a hassle just to correspond with leaders, suppliers, shareholders, and the employees as memos have to be written, edited, and submitted for approval before being disseminated. This takes time, which decreases a business's ability to respond.

With technological advanced such as the Internet and computers, communicating with everyone across the organizational chart is all easier. Now, calling the right person and sharing information is not as laborious as it was in the days of the rotary and landline phone.

This is just one of several technological changes. Such changes may be disruptive at first since businesses have to do complete overhauls of their systems but it eventually works to their favor. The more technologically advanced a company is right now, the more responsive and competitive it is in the market.

2. Customer Behavior

Back then, it was a lot (for the lack of a better word) easier to convince customers to remain loyal to a brand. That all changed in the Digital Age when people were given unprecedented access to a lot of information.

In addition, with access to information comes an increase in customer agency. Now, they feel more in control over what they want to buy or, better yet, who they want to listen to. In fact, newer generations like the Gen Y and Gen Z people can tune entire companies out if they feel that their marketing is too interruptive of their enjoyment of today's media.

As customer needs grow and evolve, so too does demand for newer things. In addition, with this demand comes opportunities for businesses to supply such. In addition, more often than not, businesses that are the first to address new needs tend to stay longer in the market.

3. The Economy

Changes in the Economy can affect businesses positively and negatively. For example, the Great Depression of the 1920s and the Recession of the 2000s caused many businesses to get shuttered and large, multimillion companies to be dissolved. This means that businesses must learn how to scale down on their operations in order to remain manageable in the hopes of becoming profitable if things stabilize.

However, a strong and secure economy does not mean that the chances of success and longevity for businesses are high. In most cases, a strong economy would lead to an increase in products and services. This means that there is a need for companies to expand which includes developing new products/services, acquiring new facilities, and hiring new staff.

Businesses have to learn how to adapt to the demands of either spectrum of economic conditions in order to survive. Fortunately, such changes do not happen exactly overnight. More often than not, experts can tell if the economy is going up or down given trends in the market. It is up to businesses to take note of these and adjust accordingly.

Why is Change Important in Leadership?

Change does bring a lot of opportunities and challenges for businesses as a whole. However, what about leaders and upper managers? What does change offer to those whose decisions ultimately shape businesses?

Change is not only occurred by changes in the environment. More often than not, it becomes necessary due to some internal issues, which may manifest in the following:

- The organization is not meeting its performance goals for a consecutive number of periods.
- The managers cannot seemingly identify new opportunities to exploit or market sectors to tap into despite major shifts in the economy.
- Mergers, acquisitions, and reorganizations have brought about new forms of businesses that have their own priorities and assets to use.
- Product and service lines are no longer responding to the needs of the customers, resulting in poor sales figures.
- The inclusion of newer, younger members of the work force with new sets of skills and workplace preferences.
- Changes in management style and standards, which may run contrary to what the company is comfortable with.

With all of these manifestations of changes, a leader must then welcome the notion of change for a number of reasons.

1. Growth for the Entire Company

Adapting to change is not just about survival. It is also about expanding and improving oneself to become more efficient and successful. Business leaders must try out new things not just to join the cause.

Perhaps change is necessary to address a long-running problem. Perhaps change is a way for the business to tap into new niches in the market. Alternatively, perhaps change is meant to boost sales from terrible to adequate to great.

Either way, change is there to push everyone in the business out of his or her comfort zones. By addressing issues that have been, simmering in the surface and disrupting the general air of comfort everyone has settled into, the workplace can become safer and more productive while also becoming less toxic.

2. Changing the Status Quo

Of course, if things go your way, your business may not see the need for change. This can be fatal for any business leader and there are ways to avoid becoming complacent (more on this later on).

However, the first important thing that any business must ask is "why?" In addition, that question must be targeted at the current standards of the business such as:

- **Current organizational layout** - How long does an act have to wait before it is approved by the higher ups? Why do you even have that much layers of management in the first place? Are things being done ASAP given the current business layout?

- **Delegation of Tasks** - If one manager is taken out of the equation, is the flow of resources and information unimpeded? What are the responsibilities of each manager in each level in the first place? Can you give responsibilities of one position and share it with others?
- **The Product** - What is the main concept of your offerings in the market? Are customers flocking to your goods or to others? Where does it stand out and why? Alternatively, why aren't your products standing out from the competition?
- **Flow of Income** - How fast does your business receive payment for products? Which departments consume the most of your company's monthly budget? Is there a way to optimize spending for every department?

Constantly asking why things are working the way they are now allows a leader to understand where things can be improved at. In addition, with this comes the opportunity for change, which leads to success.

3. Empowering Employees

Change is always uncomfortable. However, if you want such a change to become effective, everyone must have a change of paradigms. This means that even the people in the lower tiers of the organizational chart must understand the changes and positively accept it.

There are many ways to do this (which will be discussed in detail later on) but they will include the following:

- Leading by example
- Opening a transparent line of communication between heads, managers, and employees
- Incentivizing change
- Promoting a culture of accountability
- Providing training
- Accepting customer feedback

If leaders in the business are the ones, well, leading the changes, the effects that such changes will bring can circulate properly throughout the organization, bringing about massive shifts in the way that the company performs.

Think of change like a pill. If the brain (I.e. the leaders of the company) readily accept the benefits that it brings, then the body (employees) will also readily accept it and, soon enough will themselves to get rid of issues plaguing the organization for years. It is the corporate counterpart of a Placebo Effect, only a bit more tangible.

The Business Plateau: When Should You Decide to Make Changes?

It is easy to think that change is only necessary when things go bad. However, change is not only there for businesses when they are going downhill. More often than not, change is meant to keep things from even getting to that point.

As with any other field out there, there will come a point in time when you will reach a seeming peak in your business. The business has learned every trick of the trade, it has caught on to every new trend, and it has exhausted every strategy to remain relevant in the market.

Suddenly, the business stops growing and developing. Instead of a peak, you find yourself in a plateau where every development is seemingly slowly stopping. This is a naturally occurring phase in businesses and, fortunately, you can get out of this if you can make the proper decision to change at the right time.

What exactly is this Phase?

There is no exact definition for this phase in business since it is a relatively vague concept. However, to make things easier to understand, here is a visualization.

Suppose that you are a fan of a long-running movie franchise. After seeing your favorite characters conquer every challenge while learning everything that the world has to offer to them, you find yourselves watching the final movie and are now at the climax.

The heroes beat the bad person, the world is saved. End credits. Fade to black.

In addition, suddenly, you come to this realization: What are you going to do now?

This is exactly what happens when you reach this phase of your business. You have exhausted every possible strategy that you and your team could muster and have learned whatever it takes to be at the top of the market. You feel that your business cannot be fazed by anything right now.

However, that could prove to be fatal for the entire company. As such, when you are in this phase, it is best to learn when you should start applying changes here and there.

Depending on your standing in the market, this phase can hit you in two mutually exclusive ways.

A. Becoming Complacent

The dangerous thing about succeeding is that it can be rather blinding for leaders. Every success you earn takes you closer to your goals, there is no denying that. On the other hand, it can also lull you into a fall sense of security.

A common mistake businesses make when things are going their way is that they, figuratively speaking, let their guard down. They start putting less thought and effort in their strategies and operations and are confident that recognition and loyalty for the brand from their customers is enough to keep them afloat.

In addition, suddenly, there is a major shift in the economy, the market, and even customer preferences and you find yourself unable to keep up with the demands. Suddenly, every strategy you have mastered is worthless and the skills of your staff ineffective against the new wave of changes.

This is exactly what happened to many businesses who refused to acknowledge the fact that mobile devices and the Internet were more than mere novelties in the early 90s. As the Digital Age went one, these old businesses found themselves scrambling to make a living even where newer ones were thriving through the technology readily made available for all.

B. Stagnation

What if you were not exactly careless and complacent with the way you are running your business? In fact, you are paying attention to all changes happening in the market.

It is just that, for some reason, your ventures are no longer bringing in the results you want them or your company is not meeting the performance goals it has set. If you are not careful, your ventures will start hemorrhaging money for you.

This is what stagnation would look like for any business leader. It is simply the fact that the company, in its current layout or status quo, has stopped performing well in the market. It is not exactly that your products or services has dropped in quality or the overall customer experience has worsened. Your workplace is not even that tension-filled as everyone from top to bottom and from department to department are getting along with each other (at the surface, at least) It is just that reception for your offerings, or even your brand, has been rather lukewarm for a while now.

In both cases, an inability to address the shifts in customer perception and overall market behavior has been fatal for many businesses. An insistence on not fixing what they think is not broken can ultimately leave any business leader utterly incapable of bringing about meaningful changes.

In most cases, change is only possible if one adopts a new perspective and management style. For change, this means adopting a leadership style that will help the business embrace change in any shape.

Chapter II: The Basics of Change Management

What is Change Management?

To understand this new management style, it is important to define the two words respectively.

A. What is Change?

The most basic definition of Change is that it is the alteration of the status quo. As was previously mentioned, change can happen for a number of reasons, both internal and external.

Whatever the causes, change always disrupts the way things are done now in order to introduce new systems, perspectives, and solutions.

B. What is Management?

This might be elementary for experienced business leaders but the most basic definition of management is simply the execution of policies and the development of strategies in order to bring about the desired results of such execution.

To sum it up, Change Management is the execution of policies, strategies, and methods that address change happening in the market in order to produce change within the company.

Theories of Change Management

Understanding how Change Management works depends greatly on the business manager itself. In fact, different managers will apply the style depending on what theory of Change Management they lean heavily the most.

As of now, business managers acknowledge three different models to change management.

A. Kurt Lewin's Freeze Phase

Considered the godfather of the change management style, Lewin's model is perhaps the easiest to understand; and the most limiting.

For him, change is just the movement from one static phase to another. To put it in application, change is just there to disturb things in the business from time to time so that leaders and employees are not settled with their established roles and standards for too long.

B. Beer Model

On the other hand, the Beer Model is a more complex understanding of how change is brought about in the business. To put things simpler, it involves six steps wherein change is accepted and implemented. These are:

- Mobilize Commitment to Change through a Joint Diagnosis
- Develop a Shared Vision on How to Organize
- Foster Consensus, Competence, and Commitment to the Shared Vision
- Spread the Word about the Change

- Institutionalize Change through Policy Making and Development of Strategies
- Monitoring how Change is Implemented and the Results it Brings, both Foreseen and Otherwise

C. Kotter Model

Like the Beer Model, Kotter's approach towards Change Management involves several steps. However, his model involves eight instead of six. They are.

- Establishing a Sense of Urgency
- Form a Guiding, Powerful Coalition
- Creating a Vision
- Communicate the Same Vision
- Empowering Others to Act on the Vision
- Plan and Create Objectives to be Met on the Short and Long Term basis
- Consolidate Improvements
- Institutionalizing the Changes

What Is the Possible Risk with Implementing Change?

No matter how strongly you feel for the implementation of change in your business, there is always that risk that not everyone is going to be comfortable with it or, worse, do not even share your vision.

When change is not implemented in the proper manner or communicated to everyone properly, the results can be utterly devastating.

For example, workers may feel that such changes are being imposed to their detriment. Whether or not this is true, it does not change the fact that they may resist the implementation. In addition, if they find that their resistance is futile, they leave the company altogether.

As such, you are left with a greatly reduced workforce who is now required to perform in the same level to cover up the deficiency left by the vacancies. In addition, with this comes the pressure to perform which, if not handled properly, can greatly reduce morale.

Constant and honest communication, then, is necessary to allay those fears and prevent dissent from getting out of hand. When the people beneath you ask, "Hey, why are we doing this?" You must give a valid and understandable answer.

You must also be able to identify the barriers that can prevent the change from fully taking place. These include:

- Not Fully Understanding the Nature of the Change
- Lack of Competent Leadership in Implementing the Change
- Lack of Focus in Implementations
- No Engagement with Stakeholders
- Not coordinating the Change Process
- Not Recognizing Achievements in any form or magnitude
- Not Measuring Progress
- People not seeing the Results of the Change within the Promised Time Frame
- Not reviewing what has been learned in Implementing the Changes
- Progress is not Communicated

Fortunately, these barriers can be overcome through proper implementation and constant, transparent communication. Everyone needs to know that his or her contributions to the changes do matter and are valuable. This should reduce hostility and resentment in the employees as well as the fear of change.

Which Change Model Should You Use?

There is actually no right answer to this as both models are viable for applications. The Lewin model is ideal for understanding how you should consolidate changes in the system in order to bring out lasting effects in between phases.

As for the Beer and Kotter phases, they are ideal in understanding how to implement, maintain, and measure changes in the organization. As such, from this point on forward, you shall go through applying changes in your organization using principles compatible with these models.

Chapter III: Identifying Change

The first crucial step in introducing change in an organization is in identifying how change should happen. So, how does one go about changing their company?

To do this, you must know that Change can happen to any business in 3 different ways. They are as follows:

A. Developmental Change

This kind of change is implemented in order to improve current business procedures. The key here is to keep your staff well informed of such changes through constant communication as well as providing them with training in order to embrace such changes.

Some forms of Development Change include:

- Improving systems for billing, reporting, and filing of other paperwork.
- Applying updates in payroll management.
- Reforming marketing strategies and advertising efforts.

In most cases, Development Changes act as the first wave of changes that any business leader can implement in their company. They may be small and incremental in nature but they would ultimately help the business meet the demands on the market to a degree.

With developmental changes, it is necessary to manage every step of the implementation (no matter how minor) in order to make the rest of the company adopt the changes in a sensible, measured way. As such, to implement these changes, always remember to do the following.

- **Explain the Rationale** - In order for everyone to be receptive to change, they must at the very least understand why such changes need to happen.
- **Improve Their Skills** - The skill sets of everyone in the company must also be updated in order to ensure a smooth implementation of these changes.
- **Show Commitment** - If leaders themselves were seen to be applying the changes and sticking to such, the rest of the work force would follow.

B. Transitional Changes

These are the changes that companies make to replace older systems and processes with new ones. It often occurs when there are major technological and political upheavals in the market and in between businesses.

Transitional changes will include the following:

- Corporate restructuring and the creation of new divisions.
- Mergers and Acquisitions. One good example is Disney is constant buying of older companies and rivals, which includes Fox Studios, Lucas film, and Marvel Comics.
- Implementation of New Technologies.

Transitional Changes are meant to disruptive since they are replacing old structures with new ones. As such, they can be terribly uncomfortable for employees, especially for the systems that they took years to master.

As such, when implementing transitional changes, leaders need to do one thing:

Maintain an Open Line of Communication - Not only do you have to make them understand the necessity for such changes, you must also give them the assurance that such changes do not, by any means, affect the security of their jobs.

In addition, you must capture the views and contributions of your staff when implementing these changes. They must get the impression that the leadership knows that their efforts to apply such changes do matter. Of course, this means celebrating with them if such changes do lead to favorable results for everyone in the company or a department.

Lastly, you must regularly update your staff about the steps you are taking to provide them the support they need. This includes informing them of upcoming training sessions in order to adjust to the new systems.

C. Transformational Changes

This type of change is perhaps the most difficult to apply. First, it demands that you completely reshape your entire business strategy and vision, which often results to major changes in the workplace, the leadership, and the organizational chart.

Such changes can be brought about as a form of extreme response to massive changes in the market. For instance, the economy might be on a downwards trend which would compel owners and shareholders to decide to do some corporate downsizing. Paychecks will be cut, people will be laid off, departments will be shuttered, and so forth.

Transformational changes are the ones that can produce a lot of doubt and uncertainty. As such, proper management of such changes is not only recommended but also downright expected.

Some examples of transformational changes will include:

- Implementing major changes in corporate strategy and workplace culture in response to governmental pressure.
- Adopting entirely new forms of technology. One good example of this is when companies had to install servers and fiber wires as well as setting up dedicated server rooms in order to give facilities access to the Internet during the 1990s.
- Making changes in the production lineup to meet higher demands for supplies.
- Reforming and rein visioning product and service offerings in response to new competitions and to stave off massive reductions in revenue.

- Changing workplace policies to meet newer societal norms.

When implementing such changes, you must:

- **Be Strategic** - Explain to everyone how such changes would be implemented. It is impossible to implement such changes in one go. A methodical approach to implementing changes piecemeal is recommended to allow workers to mentally prepare themselves for the overall change.
- **Explain the Rationale** - This is the kind of changes that absolutely demands everyone adopt a new perspective. As such, you must continually reinforce the rationale behind the change and help your employees gradually acclimate to such changes.
- **Get Everyone Involved -** In order to curb resentment and dissent, you must let everyone join in on the discussions and continuing dialogue as well as the planning and implementing phases. The more people feel that their voices do matter before such changes are embraced; the less resistant they will be when the new status quo is being introduced.

When Should an Organization Need Change?

Not only do you have to identify the types of change you want to implement, you must also determine the reason for it. After all, the rationale of your changes will ultimately determine if people will get behind your new implementations or not.

So, when does an organization need change?

1. Poor Performance Metrics

When performance figures take a turn for the worse, this is a telltale sign that the organization needs to implement some major changes ASAP. Things like customer service statistics, production quality standards, and even financial reports are all but the end-result of a company's performance and thus reflect if a company is going on a downward or upwards trend.

Take, for example, this graph showing a company's ability to deliver orders on time.

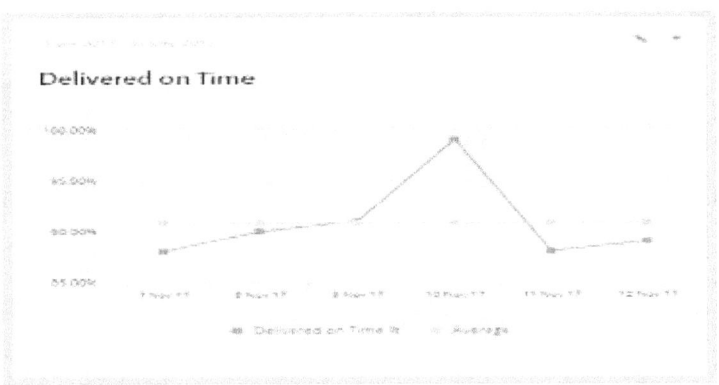

It can be understood from the graph that the company in question has constantly failed to deliver their orders on time. In fact, they have only performed satisfactorily on two dates out of five. That is not an indication of a noteworthy performance for any company.

Perhaps the problem can lie in the logistics, which would mean that some developmental and transitional changes are required. However, what if the problem of this company is a bit more embedded in its culture and the drop in on-time deliveries is but a symptom of a much larger problem?

Then, it is up to leadership to decide whether to directly address the most external manifestation (the drop in performance) or get to bottom of the problem and address the underlying issue (culture or system).

Another metric to look at is the performance of competitors. How are they faring compared to your organization? Where are they succeeding and where are you not? More often than not, the milestones of your competitors can tell you whether the organization you run needs to experience a major overhaul.

2. Workplace Issues

Just how exactly is everyone getting along in your company? One major indicator that your company needs change is a high turnover rate in the work force. This is a telltale sign that satisfaction in employees is that low that they would rather seek their fortunes elsewhere.

A. Low Morale

What you have to remember is that a motivated work force can manifest productively. If they love what they are doing and are rewarded for going beyond what is required for them, your employees would do anything to stay in the company.

Movement through the ranks is also a telltale sign of the overall health of the workplace. If the people above do not change much in their positions while those below are stuck at certain positions for too long, then there is a clear discrepancy and divide between employees and managers.

In addition, low employee moral does negatively affect the performance of the company as a whole. If they were not rewarded for putting in the extra effort, why would employees go beyond for you? As such, it is expected to see a gradual decline in production quality and overall workforce performance if the problem is not addressed.

B. Increase in Workplace Incidents

However, a more pressing indicator of the need for changes in the workplace is an increase in employee discomfort and even accidents in the workplace. This is a telltale sign that the facility itself is degrading and a major transitional change in its layout is necessary.

Aside from accidents, there might also be an increase of tensions between workers, managers, and supervisors. There might be an increase of issues regarding workplace harassment and other employee abuses. These would indicate that the workplace itself is no longer an area conducive to the development of personal skills as well as innovations for the company.

C. Incompetent Leaders

Challenges in the business are always changing but there is the chance that the persons you place in charge of managing the minutiae of your business are not keeping pace. The development in leadership is often overlooked when implementing changes but is one that ultimately shapes the course of the company from that point on moving forward.

Leaders must know how to bring out the best of their employees through coaching and encouragement. If they themselves contribute to the toxicity of the workplace, then it is time for a restructuring in order to plug the gap between the leadership and the workforce.

3. Management Issues

Even if your management is good at identifying opportunities, perhaps they are not quick enough to act on it. As was stated a few chapters before, complacency is equally fatal to the business as incompetence as it gets in the way of taking action that is effective.

When videogame publisher Konami decided to make some changes in their leadership in the 2010s, they did so with the intention of making the company efficient while also addressing seemingly poor sales figures.

However, the way that their leadership went about implementing these changes were poorly received. From becoming too oppressive in monitoring employee communications and break times to even imposing harsh penalties and demotions for the smallest of infractions, it was apparent that something was clearly wrong within the way the company is dealing with internal issues.

In addition, Konami had a much publicized falling out with one of their primary contributors, developer Hideo Kojima, which led to the latter is termination from the company. But instead of softening the transition to the new status quo, Konami decided to handle the matter in a publicly disastrous way by providing stipulations that limited Kojima's and several other's ability to find employment in the market.

To keep things short, Konami's series of managerial missteps resulted in backlash after backlash from the public, which resulted in worse sales figures and even worse employee morale.

A good manager needs to address issues on eliminating waste, improve production quality, and quelling employee dissent. They should also have the initiative to recommend changes in the workplace, especially the ones that upper leadership have yet to identify.

An inability to do any of these is a major indicator that the culture of your company no longer supports a drive towards innovation. If employees are not encouraged to do better and management itself is not doing any measures to foster a healthy relationship between all departments of the company, then the organization's ability to be responsive to outside opportunities is severely limited.

4. Inability to Respond to Outside Change

Perhaps the biggest indicator that your organization needs of change is if it is way behind the times. Is the technology optimized to new standards? Is the workplace designed in a way that it follows new labor standards? Is your production facilities following the most recent standards in environmental conservation and protection? Is information spread through your organization through email or the old-fashioned way?

There is nothing that inherently bad in doing things the way that you are most comfortable with. However, the world has been moving on without your company this major indicator. If not addressed, your company and whatever it offers might just become obsolete.

A change in your company culture has a strong potential to refocus and re-energize your company. The addition of new, younger faces in your organization and the acquisition of faster and more efficient equipment is a good start in making your company keep up with the world around it.

To Summarize

Knowing what changes need to be done and how to make them take effect is just the first step in transforming your company into a responsive entity. Regardless of how big the transformation is, you must understand that there will always be challenges and potential pitfalls that you and your team will encounter in implementing these.

In fact, you should find a balance between optimizing your company's current assets while also addressing areas that do need improvement. This way, you can keep your company focused on its primary goals while also becoming all the more adaptable.

However, change is not something that can be done if you yourself are not guided by something. Even the loftiest of ideals or the most intangible of concepts can help companies achieve results that are as real as they are long lasting.

For this, you need to construct a vision for your company. A vision that is geared towards making things move ever forward.

Chapter IV: Crafting a Vision for Change

What is a Vision?

The best description of what a vision is that it is a mental picture of what is to come. It is a construct in the mind that depicts what the future can bring to a person or his organization, although it has not yet happened.

It is simply the embodiment of what a person aspires for and what is possible if enough effort is exerted. It, to put it in simpler terms, is the very thing that compels people to act and guides their every decision.

In addition, this does beg the question: Why do leaders need to come up with a vision? To answer that, one must understand what having a vision does and brings to the organization as a whole.

1. It Gives Direction

Leaders may be expected to plant their feet firmly in the Now but they are also expected to see several steps ahead of everybody else. This is actually important, as a vision not only molds what people must do now to see the results in the future but to also avert potential catastrophes.

A vision is what keeps a leader focused especially if things are currently hard while also helping them plan. The moment that you envision success for your organization is the moment that you actually lay the foundations for that group to eventually achieve its goals.

2. It Provides Motivation

The hardest things to do, as a leader is to remain committed to something even if things are seemingly not going their way. Morale can be a rather expensive commodity in businesses especially in major economic downturns.

If the leaders start to lose faith in the cause, the people beneath them would waver. However, leaders that do press on can be seen as a major source of inspiration for everyone that follows them.

However, of course, the vision that the leader carries must be strong and compelling enough to motivate other people. If it is based on purely lofty ideals that are not tempered with a bit of reality and practicality, it itself might falter under hard times.

3. It Drives us Forward

When the leadership is driven by a strong vision, they are unfazed by every set back and minor inconvenience that pops up along the way. This is because what they envision is compelling enough to make them stand their ground and take one more step even if everything is pushing back.

A driven leader will make sure that everyone contributes to meeting every goal in every phase of the plan and persevere until the end goal is in sight. They understand that everything that was ever planned for the business is achievable with a whole lot of perseverance and teamwork.

This is why commanders personally leading charges in ancient battlefields were seen as major morale boosters. Nothing can compel a man to press on towards the unknown than a leader who is brave enough to set an example, after all.

4. It Provides Focus

With a lot of distractions and priorities all vying for a leader's attention nowadays, it can be hard for any leader to get things done. By acting on one's vision, however, it gives them focus which makes them see what needs to be done and what can be put off for, say, another few days or so.

A vision will help a leader create a timetable as to what goals should be achieved first. This way, they can quickly scratch off every goal in the plan as quickly as possible without being stuck doing mundane and ultimately useless tasks.

It also helps a leader delegate. By showing them how much of the tasks they can do and what they can delegate to people who have the better skills to complete such, a vision can help a leader make sure that their organization completes its goals in the soonest possible time.

5. It Gives Meaning and Purpose

Most important of all, a Vision helps a leader answer the question "why are we doing all of this". If you are to implement a change, people will naturally ask what the purpose is for all of this. It can be hard to answer that question if you do not know yourself why the organization has to implement such changes.

However, with a vision, you can understand why change needs to happen for the organization. In addition, when you come to that realization, all that is left to do is to communicate what you have realized in a way that everyone else will see the point too.

Having the Right Mentality as a Leader!

This might sound as clichéd but there are many things in running in business, which are matters of the mind. In fact, even the best laid plans and best of intentions a leader could have for a business will never be sustainable if they do not have the motivation or the focus.

So how important is it for a leader to adopt the right positive mentality when running an organization? The short answer is "very". However, let us expound on that.

Why Dreamers are Successful

A dream is similar to a vision, a goal without a set time. It may or may not become true (depending on who you ask) and it is often the first thing to change when Reality sets in.

When plans are set back, deals and partnerships go awry, and mishap after mishap occurs, you might realize that your original vision for the business is gone or, at least, has been greatly altered. Becoming cynical after so many years running an organization is a pitfall many leaders can fall into and it can be fatal for everyone else in the company.

However, there are reasons why you should maintain the perspective of a dreamer at all times. They are the following:

1. What You Think, You Manifest

There is this saying that whatever a business leader thinks often becomes a self-fulfilling prophecy. Why is this so? It is because one's thoughts are simply concepts that have yet to be realized by the person. To put it in fancier terms, your dream or vision is just a prelude to reality.

History has no shortage of examples of how people turned their dreams into actual reality. The automobile started out as an engine propped on a cart. The Disney Company we see today started out as one man's scribble of a cartoon mouse. In essence, the biggest and most successful companies and concepts you see today started out as mere thoughts but were eventually expressed into real objects.

If you need further convincing, you just need to look at the tactics employed by car salespersons. They know that every person has a dream and so, instead of selling people cars, they are selling them "tools" to make those dreams into reality.

This is why the best way to seal a deal when it comes to cars is to make the customer through a test drive. Once a person knows that their dream can be realized, the deal is as good as done.

2. A Strong Focus Alters Your Perspective

Visions can give you a certain focus, which ultimately change the way you perceive things. For example, a business leader that focuses too much on the tiresome aspects of the organization tends to have opinions that revolve around the concept of businesses as nothing but repetitive busywork.

However, a leader that focuses on the vision they set for the organization sees things differently. They see opportunities where others see potential failure. They see not only the business as what it is now but also what it can become through effort.

The point is that dreamers have a strong focus, which, in turn, can affect the overall direction of the organization. Sure, nothing about running a business is ever easy. There are just too many things that could go wrong at a single instance, forever changing the viability of that venture. However, those that do dream big tend to also achieve greater levels of success than those that remain cynical.

3. Impossibility is Impossible

When it comes to dreamers, the word "impossible" is not part of their vocabulary. The closest thing one gets to that word is "I'm Possible". A focused person cares too much about the goal that any impediment or obstacle that comes their way are approached with a determination to overcome.

In addition, since everything becomes possible for a dreamer, then it means that dreamers also tend to recover quickly from every setback they encounter. For them, problems that would otherwise cripple any business is just an opportunity to discover an alternate route towards achieving a goal. It does not matter how long or how hard achieving a goal would become. All that matters is that they get there.

These are just some of the things that make a dreamer a good leader in any organization. In fact, this mindset can be a great asset if you happen to find yourself running a business now. Do remember that there is nothing easy when it comes to achieving success. Without the right perspective, however, any organization would lose its way in the market and ultimately not achieve the purpose it was put up in the first place for.

Creating an Actionable Vision

Having a vision is easy. The challenge comes from framing that vision into something that is achievable, easy to understand, and actionable through the strategies that your company could come up to make that dream into a reality.

In essence, it is in the Execution where the quality of your Vision for the company will be determined. In order to make your vision easy to attain, there are few tips that you have to remember when creating it.

1. Keep Things Simple

The primary reason why visions become long lists of impossible and lofty goals is that the ones making it take everything in at once. For example, if your vision for change is to make the organization into a multinational conglomerate of companies that use the latest technology in whatever industries you operate in; of course, it is going to look daunting for anyone reading it.

To make the dream a bit more achievable, you have to lay out the path towards it. To reach the destination, you have to chart the course.

So, how do you go about turning your company from this state to that state? You have to identify the phases that the business is going to go through when implementing the vision. The first phase might include overhauling the systems of the company, the second phase might include acquiring new assets and making mergers with other companies, the third phase might include buying out the competition and looking for other opportunities for expansion.

In essence, you turn the one big Vision into a series of achievable steps that people can focus their energies on, one-step at a time.

2. Set it in Writing

This might be elementary but writing your goals is a crucial step in turning your dreams into reality. The reason for this is actually quite simple: when you write things down, you are subconsciously telling your brain to never, ever forget this piece of information.

Of course, how goals are written tend to affect how the brain interprets it. When writing your vision and mission, it is necessary to use assertive words like "Must", "Shall", and "Will" as they assume a commanding and direct tone. On the other hand, words like "Like" and "Want" may show desire but they lack determination. If possible, be as direct and commanding when framing your vision for the rest of the group.

Then there is the need to maintain a positive tone for your vision. For example, if you envision the business lasting for another 5 years, write something along the lines of "the organization will expand its operations and maintain financial security within a period of 5 years".

Do not write it in a manner that the reader will see the overall message, as "We don't want to be bankrupt within a few years". In addition, once this vision is written and accepted by everybody else, you must then put it in somewhere where it is going to be visible at all times.

3. Set Some Contingencies

The hardest element to deal with when planning for an organization is the Unknown. There are too many variables and unforeseen circumstances present in any organization that it can leave someone with negative psychological effects. If you think that there are many margins for error in a plan, you tend to become cynical.

However, this can be easily remedied by planning for contingencies. How to do this is quite simple: For every decision you make, think of the worst possible scenario that might arise out of that decision.

Once you have identified the worst, you can gradually come up with solutions on how to address such. Not only will this help you avoid such problems in every phase of your plan for the organization, it also subconsciously helps by reminding you that you are always in control; even if things go wrong.

4. Stick to the Plan

Even if you are on the lookout for worst possible scenarios, it is still necessary that you commit yourself to the plan. Remember that setting a vision for the business is not just a way to help the organization achieve a purpose. It is there to remind everyone what they are supposed to do, where everyone is currently with respect to the plan, and what has been achieved so far.

With this, everybody will be on the same page and can be reminded what they are supposed to do next.
By making your vision actionable, even on paper, you set your organization in a position where it is the most capable of achieving that goal piece by piece. Keep in mind that strategies might change in response to shifts in the market but whatever goal you have set up will remain the same and will be achieved in form or another.

When Optimism is Hard

There is no escaping the fact that there are times when running an organization can get difficult. Aside from issues in performance as well as the company culture itself, you would also have to deal with negativity.

Emotions like anxiety and depression can kill the momentum of any change you are trying to implement. It can even make such implementation near impossible in the first place. The reason for this is that negative emotions do not necessarily attack the systems in the organization, things that changes can effectively address. It targets the people running it.

However, before anything else, there are two things that you have to know about negativity. First, it can be reduced and eliminated through a series of processes over a considerable period.

Second, in as much as negativity can become prevalent, it does not effectively change the direction of the business. It is up to the leader to determine whether they let their negative thoughts run them or they manage their thoughts properly.

In addition, if you do choose to address that negativity when creating a vision for your business, there are some tips that you have to remember.

A. Accept that a Problem Exists

The first step towards recovery is acknowledging the fact that there is something wrong and that it needs to be fixed. Fortunately, for you, negativity is not exactly subtle when manifesting itself in the work place. You can see it by the way people act or, if you need incontestable facts, in the figures.

Look at this chart, for example.

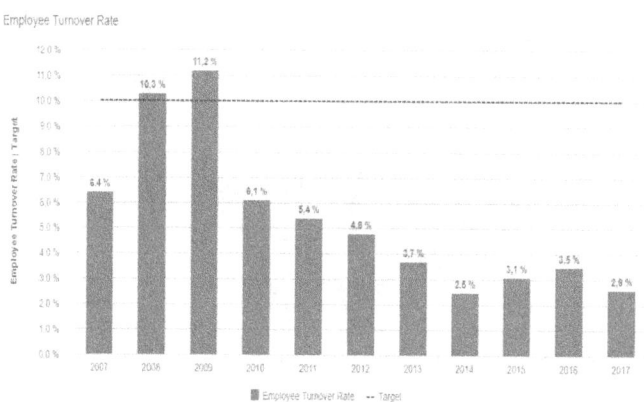

To anyone else, the graph might just be tallying the turnover rates of employees over the years. To anyone that looks deeper, however, the graph does show a pattern that directly links to the company culture.

What made turnover rates go beyond the 10.00% threshold during 2008 and 2009? What caused the upwards spike in between 2007 and 2008? Perhaps this might imply that there is something wrong in the workplace, which caused employees to leave the company in droves for those two years.

In addition, apparently, the problem was addressed starting from 2010 as turnover rates have decreased drastically in the years that followed. However, this would not have been possible if upper management did not at the very least acknowledged that something was wrong in the first place.

B. Ease Up on the Tension

In some instances, the negativity cannot be addressed if you put more pressure. Running an organization is going to take a toll on anybody, psychologically and emotionally. As such, all it takes is one more push for everything to snap and the once underlying problem is now out in the happen and harder to control.

The trick in dealing with negativity in the workplace, then, is to keep a healthy state of mind. Remember that your effectiveness as a leader is utterly depending on your perspective towards things.

If you take a step back, you give yourself enough of a breather to recollect your thoughts. Perhaps giving yourself a small break can let you see the problem from a different perspective. In addition, this should allow you to come up with a better vision to implement longer-lasting changes in your organization.

C. Rally the Troops

In some cases, negativity and tensions at the workplace comes not from the fact that there is a problem. Technically speaking, the managers and leaders in your organization may be aware that a problem exists and that it needs proper addressing.

However, what they do not agree on is the way that it should be addressed. For example, if the company has problems with production quality, there would be some that would think that changing the facility's layout or technology would solve it. Others would think that retraining old employees would do the trick. Then there are some that think that downsizing operations would solve the problem.

For one problem, the company's managers have come up with three different solutions. So which one is the best? There is actually no direct answer to that but how you respond to the dilemma, as the overall leader would matter.

The best way to rally everybody into one direction, then, is to find common ground. One group sees things from a production perspective. The other group see the problem from a workforce-centric perspective. In addition, the third group sees things from an efficiency-based perspective.

You can unite all the different approaches, then, by reminding everyone that all options are valid. However, the best one is a comprehensive one that addresses all external and core issues.

To do that, you need to remind everybody of the vision of the company. Better yet, you introduce a new one that embraces change while remaining true to the values and intentions of the original.

By coming up with a newer and shared vision, leaders can effectively consolidate every effort that everyone is expected to give to meet a common goal. In addition, if everybody agrees on something, the organization can quickly meet its goals and ultimately achieve that goal.

Chapter V: Understanding Organizational Behavior Towards Change

When trying to implement change into an organization, one must understand how that organization takes change. More specifically, how does an entity made up by different people with its own hierarchy and policies react towards something that is as foreign as change?

Understanding how your organization may or may not behave when introduced to something new can tell you if such changes were to be successful if implemented. However, of course, this could tell you how you may guide them be more accepting towards the new and unknown without straying off the values and vision that made the company that it is today.

What is Organizational Behavior?

The best definition of organizational behavior is that it refers to the way people behave as an individual or as part of a group within an organization. Each action that an individual make, overt and subtle, can eventually mold the culture of the company, which, in turn, affects the other aspects, that make up that organization.

By extension, organizational behavior affects how well a company performs and maintains its presence in the market. It may be exhibited by the employees or acknowledged by the leadership up top. It may even be consciously accepted or rejected by everyone within the group or parts of it.

Either way, so as long as it is expressly manifested, how an organization behaves as its own entity will ultimately prove to be an asset or a liability when the need for change arises.

Management and Organizational Behavior

Given how pivotal individual and group behavior can change the way a company performs, it is important that the leaders of a company understand and define their own group's organizational behavior.

They must understand how the attitudes of an individual would translate into their performance within the company and, in turn, their overall productivity as a member of a larger entity. However, this analysis is not only limited towards one person.

Group dynamics should also be taken into consideration, as the organization is expected work as one cohesive person.

Also, in order for the entire organization to move and work at optimum levels, managers must also find ways to quickly resolve conflicts and encourage employees to positively contribute to a more productive company culture.

How a person adapts to their workplace will also play a key role in the overall organizational behavior. In order to properly motivate the workforce, a manager must understand how a person copes with their tasks and come up with decisions crucial to their work.

It is important to understand that a workforce can only operate as smoothly as possible if the executives can motivate them and design a workplace that is conducive to their development and productivity.

To sum it up, a nuanced appreciation of what ultimately composes organizational behavior and how it is manifested will help managers develop their own style that is compatible to that culture. Once they do that, they can guide the company to be more responsive and accepting of the prospect change.

What Gets Affected by Change?

Although every organization has their own way of behaving around change, change itself can target the same key areas within every company.

A. The Technology

This would include the more tangible, mechanical, and procedural aspects of the business. A change may affect the overall state of machinery, the production process, and even the delivery of services and goods to clients.

This would also include other systems that the company relies on to function properly. Change may also affect how people communicate with each other, how documents are prepared and submitted, and how people get access to the information that they need.

B. The Product and Service

Perhaps the most direct manifestation (or result) of change, the overall appearance, quality, and composition of one's own offerings to the market would be different once changes are implemented. For example, an organization might introduce a new product line or resurrect a defunct one.

In most cases, the product or service library would just be expanded to accommodate new niches in the market or to tap into new demographics that the company has discovered.

C. Administration and Management

In order to affect long lasting changes in the company's culture, the guiding forces behind the company must also be change. The mission and vision statement, for example, might be changed in order to respond to the challenges of the time and even policies that have been with the company ever since its birth would be repealed by new ones.

Of course, the observable change in this regard would be the very composition of its leaders. People up top might be removed and replaced with fresh faces, new divisions might be formed to tap into new segments of the market, and people once belonging to the employee class might be elevated to positions of management and policy-making.

D. The Workforce and Human Resource

If the organization of the people up top change, so will the layout of the people at the bottom. For instance, if a new division is created, people will be taken from their current departments and placed there since the leadership feels that their skills are the most suitable there. Of course, this leaves a vacuum in their former departments, which have to be filled with new people.

The relationship between the employees, the managers, and shareholders might also be changed in this regard. For instance, the government might come up with new labor laws, which requires the company to update its policies for employees.

In as much as these changes are significant, the effects they bring are also not mutually exclusive. A change in one area will ultimately lead to change in another. For example, a change in equipment can change the quality of the product and the workplace, as people have to be retrained to operate it.

Alternatively, a change in leadership will also result in the change in company vision, which ultimately ends with a change in the product or service library. Alternatively, a change in company vision might give rise to the introduction of new departments, which in turn creates new positions that need filling in.

Resisting Change

As was stated, Change is disruptive by nature. It is not something that is immediately comfortable or appreciated until the tangible benefits can be experienced.

In fact, the things that ultimately shaped the human experience of the 20th and 21st century either was met with indifference at best or disdain at worst.

When the Television was first introduced, cinema mogul Darryl Zanuck laughed at the idea and boldly declared that the world will eventually get tired of starting at a "plywood box". The dependence of entertainment today on the principles built by the television would prove that he was sorely mistaken.

The same thing happened when Henry Ford built the automobile and his lawyer told him that horse-drawn carriages were here to stay. Alternatively, more recently, what about Steve Ballmer of Microsoft who declared in 2007 that the iPhone would not get any mileage in the market. Their resistance to changes were ultimately proven rather myopic.

One key characteristic you have to understand about human beings is that we are the happiest when things are comfortable and familiar. The avoidance of pain and frustration as well as social rejection is deeply embedded into the human psyche that it remains a strong driving force in us today, whether we are aware of it or not.

So what happens when a visionary tells everybody that what he or she are doing is wrong or that another, better way is available? People will naturally resist. Even an employee who is promoted to a new position with more responsibilities will face the change with at least an iota of fear and stress.

It is not just the employees that even resist change. In fact, everybody in the organization will be apprehensive towards it, even for a bit. Look at this graph below.

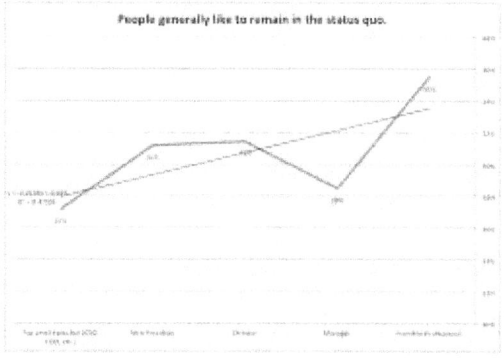

It might show that the trend for resistance to change goes upward the lower one gets to the organization chart but the point is that everybody within the group can expressly or impliedly show their resistance to what is new, untested, and unknown. The status quo, after all, provides the comfort and security they need in order to thrive under the umbrella of the organization.

Since resistance is part of the human behavior, a manager must understand then how to manage such so that the changes they are to implement will ultimately become part of the company culture.

How is Resistance Manifested?

The organization, as was established, is made up of different individuals and groups. As such, resistance is going to be manifested at three different levels across the entire company.

1. Organizational Resistance

In this instance, it is the organization as a whole that outright rejects the change and push towards maintaining the status quo.

This usually happens in long-running companies who feel that they are the most successful, or stable, if they insist on doing the things that they are familiar with.

Therefore, the entire company would give the impression of inflexibility and therefore cannot adapt to demands of change from the outside world and its internal systems.

This might be attributed to what is called as corporate inertia. The constant push and pull from different conflicting factions within the company can lead to infighting as well as poor business decisions. Out of fear that one group would prevail over the other, the leadership would make decisions that seemingly keep the playing field equal but, in turn, would impede the organization's ability to move forward with the changing world.

How Does One Curb Organizational Resistance?

This all boils down to the company's inherent reward system as well as its company culture. Companies that promote a high level of trust and cooperation between groups often lay down the foundations for which change can become ultimately possible.

For instance, the mere enactment of policies where employees are rewarded for coming up with new ideas or that managers are constantly trained to better manage the people and facilities assigned to them can subtly change the people's perception towards change.

Since everything is moving forward but the company remains devoted to its core values, then everyone in the organization would see that change does not have to come at the expense of losing what makes the company unique. As a result of seeing change as not detrimental to the security of their jobs, people at all levels of the organization would readily welcome a more dynamic company culture.

Another issue to address here is Timing. If the company is still adjusting to changes, the last thing any leader would do is to shake up the status quo again by introducing changes; especially changes that directly address the changes previously implemented.

If one were to do that, employees and managers would most likely voice their resistance towards change. As such, you must think about how you go about implementing change to ease the workforce to the new standard.

2. Group Resistance

Groups tend to form because the people that make them up found the value of coordinating all their efforts to meet a common goal. As such, that group has become its own self-sustaining community with its own norms and dynamics. As such, to change the makeup of that group would be to change what makes it unique. As such, resistance is to be expected.

One good example to this is what happened to The Beatles. Right at the end of the group's life, there were already simmering tensions brought about by creative differences. However, for most of the time, their arguments would be settled by a talk and the others would immediately pull the one that feels left behind. Of course, everyone was expected to contribute and every contribution they made were personally attributed to them.

This all changed when someone new in the form of Yoko Ono was introduced to the group. As she had a closer emotional bond to John Lennon than his friends did, any act she would do in relation to the group's cohesion was seen as an interference to what made the group unique. Sad to say, the Beatles were forever disbanded and some personal grievances remain not addressed even to this day.

So, if a group used to practicing a centralized form of decision making is told to decentralize it, what would be the most logical reaction that group members would make? They would resist as such change goes directly against to what they are doing.

How to Address Group Resistance

In order to make a group accepting towards change, you must directly address the elements that make the group cohesive in the first place. If a group is to be disbanded in favor of a different structure, you can expect the core members to be resistant to that change.

However, that group cohesion can be used to your advantage. For instance, if you give the group a bit of agency on how to implement such changes, they would be less resistant to such since leadership is respecting their cohesion.

By giving the group the ability to implement change in a way they see fit, you can gradually overcome their resistance. Even the resistance of a single member can be overcome using the group's centralized decision-making process. You may not have completely removed dissent but, at the very least, you have won most of that group over to your side.

3. Individual Resistance

On a personal level, change is uncomfortable due to the direct consequences it brings. With change comes the need to learn new things and adapt to new conditions. For instance, when the desktop computer was introduced to the workplace in the late 1980s, many felt apprehensive at learning how to adjust to the keyboard when they were previously used to the typewriter.

However, there are some fears, which may be justified at a personal level. If the person feels that their job is at risk due to the change, or if they do not fully trust the management regardless of the assurance the latter offers to them, they would naturally be resistant to such changes.

Sometimes, the individual's inherent traits make them resistant to change. Their culture, personality, and experience can ultimately shape their ability to accept change.

Encouraging Change

Resistance can be encountered at every level of the organization. In fact, you may have to deal with multiple forms of resistance at any given time. So how you are going to curb that resistance and get everyone on board? Here are a few tactics that could help you.

A. Education and Proper Communication

Resistance is brought about by a fear of the unknown. As such, a leader should address that with information. You should have meetings with your other leaders and shareholders who will then disseminate the information to the people under their charge.

Constant memorandums, updates, and even newsletters can help address such fears and make people understand the rationale behind the change. Of course, there is the chance that people might still misinterpret what you are trying to implement but misinformation is easily overcome through transparency.

B. Becoming Involved

People resist because they feel that they do not have any say on the matter. To avoid this, you should make everyone involved in applying the change. When introducing the change, give employees the time to process such changes and air out their concerns or ideas.

By letting people know that their voices matter, you give them a sense of agency on how things should move forward from this point on. The obvious disadvantage to this is that it is time consuming and you are relinquishing a bit of your control over the change to your employees. However, resistance is often quelled when people realize that they can ultimately mold how things are going to be.

C. Support

This is highly effective against individual resistance as it allows you to personally deal with the concerns a single person has over the changes. Do they feel that they are going to be replaced by someone else? Give them the assurance that their job remains secure as ever?

Do they feel that they cannot adjust to the new machines and standards? A retraining program might do the work. The point is that if an individual's personal concerns were met, they would be less hesitant towards change. As an added bonus, you have won that employee over since the company actually took the time to address his concerns.

D. Negotiations

This strategy is also dependent on your ability to give agency towards others for the change. For instance, you are about to expand on your facility and add in new employees. Such changes will be met with resistance by existing labor unions as they feel that it would affect the cohesion of their group and even the securities of their individual jobs.

Talking with the Labor Unions and addressing their concerns will be a good start but you might want to consider adding in incentives and trade-offs to sweeten the deal. Appearing negotiable during dialogues with your managers and employees gives the impression that such changes are possible to implement and do not necessarily come at the expense of others.

Of course, the major disadvantage with this strategy is time and money. Negotiations can take time to be finished, time otherwise spend on implementing changes. However, there is the chance that you might find a superior alternative method of implementing such changes, an alternative where everybody ultimately wins.

E. Coordination and Manipulation

If resistance to change is strong in the workforce, you can employ a bit of diversion to make them willingly agree to the changes. This is a rather underhanded tactic as you are diverting their attention from the main issue by manufacturing a need that your change will ultimately answer.

For instance, you are about to build a new facility but the labor union fears that you may renege on the terms. To distract them, you might have some outside people "create" a distraction on the current site by harassing the people there.

Once tensions are high, you will then arrive to dispel the situation and offer the union a lucrative option that will prevent such harassment from occurring again.

As was stated, this strategy is highly dependent on your ability to deceitfully manipulate others and hide such fact. If you were to be discovered, mistrust will drop to an all-time low, which may never recover so as long as you are the leader of the organization.

As such, it is of the best interest of everyone that you never, ever resort to this tactic. In fact, the only reason this strategy is included here is not that it is valid and legal. Instead, it is here to inform you what happens if you do resort to using this on your organization.

F. Force

If time is of the essence, you can just plow through the implementations; dissent and concerns be damned. This method is rather quick as it is effective as you can save time while still implementing your new vision for the organization.

The downside is that you do not give time for everybody to commit to the change. What happens, then, is that the changes do not last long. Soon enough, people will go back to their old ways or find ways to cut corners in the new standards.

To Summarize

How the organization ultimately behaves when faced with the prospect of change can be dependent on how you present your offer and how much you involve everyone in implementing the changes. You can even use a combination of all the tactics above (minus the fifth, of course) to make people in the organization support your intentions.

The point here is that leaders must ultimately respect the fact that the organization is an independent entity. It may not accept your proposal of change but it can be reasoned with. If you make it see the value of what you are trying to bring to the organization, resistance can be curbed in all of its levels.

Chapter VI: Defining (and Refining) Your Management Style

Many in the work force would agree on the notion that they do not leave companies because the company is going downhill. They leave because of the people running it are terrible at their jobs.

The life of the company and security of those that work on it are utterly dependent on the decisions of the leadership. To put it in other words, what you decide to do and how you even treat the people underneath the organizational chart will ultimately make or break the business.

Fortunately, for you, your management style is easily observable. This means that properly identifying such a style and how you can hone it for the good of the company would result in tangible results.

What Is Your Management Style?

First things first. How do you fashion yourself as a leader? Not every leader out there has the same style and approach towards running their business.

However, what you should know is this: no style is truly good or bad. It is how you use that leadership style that will determine whether you succeed or fail as a leader. Understanding your style and how it can have an impact on those that follow you, then, would be crucial to your company embracing change.

As of now, managers and leaders use five distinct styles when managing their businesses and employees.

1. The Autocrat

This is perhaps one of the oldest management styles and is used by a leader who believes on the notion of "It's my way or the highway". This style is highly effective in environments that absolutely require no margin of error. As such, people with a military or emergency service based background tend to use this style as a default.

For Autocrats, the rules are absolute. As such, they dictate all methods and processes and expect everybody just to follow. Inputs from others, for them, are unnecessary and rarely solicit such.

In your traditional factory setting, this management style would have found a home. Other major people are also known to use the style such as Vince Lombardi of the Green Bay Packers and Sam Walton, founder of Walmart.

However, autocratic styles are like spices: they are only good in small, controlled doses. Too much of this "take it or leave" style to running your employees is not going to work well in prolonged periods as employees right now do value a leader who knows when to step back and let others do the heavy lifting too.

So when can an autocratic style be best if you are not naturally inclined to it? It may be best in emergencies such as the company experiencing the worst effects of a local economic downturn. Perhaps a leader who can tell people what to do and micromanage every minutiae of the business might just prove to be an effective guide for the company during tense situations.

However, if the situation demands that you ease up on the pressure, it is best to resort to other management styles.

2. The Coach

The key focus for this leader is the word "Growth". This style is heavily favored in businesses right now as it naturally inclined towards making people develop on their strengths and improve on their weaknesses.

The coach believes on the idea of Leadership by Example. In fact, their most used phrase would go along the line of "hey, let me show you things are done".

This is the exact style used by Andrew Carnegie when he developed and trained nobodies into managerial roles. One of those trainees was Charles Schwab who became the first president of US Steel.

The key to success with this managerial style is to develop a close relationship with those around you. Building rapport with your employees and managers can help you understand what they are good or lacking at.

After all, not all that coaching would do you any good if the people around you feel that you are insincere or seemingly disconnected with your interactions with them.

3. The Friend

Daniel Goleman developed this management style in 2002. In here, the focus is harmony on the workplace with not just people of the same level or position but between everyone in different departments and levels.

Here, the People are put first, not the Mission. This might sound counterproductive to the goals of implementing change in the organization but you have to think about it this way: if there is no synergy between the agents of change (the people), any change that you want to implement would be ineffective.

As such, this management style is ideal in elevating the workplace, which, in turn, could lead to a change in company culture. If the workforce is engaged, they are more susceptible to the notion of change.

However, this management style is sorely lacking on the field of accountability. If everybody is your friend, how are you supposed to make him or her stand by his or her word? Suppose that one member of your company does something that damages the company or its bottom line. Can they be penalized or would you let your friendship prevail.

The key to honing this style, then, is in finding a balance. People should focus on forging a relationship that allows them to work better, not just be people they hang out with. This way, the work that needs to be done is done and workplace synergy is all the better for it.

Joe Torre, former manager of the New York Yankees, used this style to a great degree. He often recognized the contributions of individual players and celebrated with them in all wins. However, He was also not the one to make excuses if the team fails and puts everyone to task on improving themselves so the next game results in win for the team.

4. The Democrat

With this leadership style, a leader makes it a point to let everyone join in and contribute to the effort. As such, it is a direct opposite to the autocratic leadership style as decision making now is less centralized.

Here, a leader gives everyone a sense of agency and ownership with the project. As a result, everyone would take pride in his or her work, which leads to a more motivated workforce. In essence, the focus on this style is Employee Engagement.

A democratic leader, when making decisions, always ask this question: What is the Pleasure of the Body? Soon enough, everyone would offer his or her ideas, which, after further brainstorming, would coalesce into a strategy that everybody can get behind with. In addition, since this strategy is everybody's baby, they are now more committed to seeing things through.

The key to success with this leadership style, then, is to relinquish a bit of your control and give it your staff. For some, however, that is not easy to do especially if they have been in the position for a long time and have held tied their responsibilities closely to their identity. However, with an open mind or a sense of urgency, you can realize the value of letting a bit of that power go.

Steve Jobs used this management style when he was brought back to Apple in the mid-1990s. Instead of calling all the shots, he found it more prudent to hire people who may excel in some fields more than he may and provided them with the resources to express their ideas into tangible products.

The result was that the pool of information that he could draw as a leader was widened and the combined experience of the Apple leadership considerably expanded. Due to that style, Apple managed to gain a foothold in more segments and markets and continues to do so even today, despite Steve's passing.

5. The Pace Setter

This style is known by other names such as the Frontline General, the Servant Leader, the Sprinter, and the Leader by Example. Here, the leader establishes the standards and sets the pace for everybody else to follow.

The pace setter is the kind of leader who does not tell people what to do nor do they show them how to do it. They live and breathe their own standards in the hopes that people will see the value of such and follow suit.

As a direct result, the Pace Setter obsesses over doing things better and faster and will ask the same to live up to the same standard. They are quick to identify poor performers and stragglers, demands more from these people, and, if these people continuously fail to rise up to the occasion, do things himself.

This management style is a rather strong motivator as it makes everyone move in the same pace as the leader. After all, how you are supposed to contribute if everybody else is already moving several paces in front of you?

However, as much as this style is great for motivation, it can be exhaustive. Not everyone can see the value of living to the same standards and thus would be more insistent on doing things their way.

Thus, this style is great only in short bursts and is utterly dependent on the company's existing culture. Leaders who want to use this style must first determine if the conditions are right for application. If the times do not call for an all-out sprint, then it is prudent to resort to other management styles.

This style is also dependent on the leader's energy levels. A leader who is more reserved and cautious is not going to be find this style comfortable. Alternatively, a leader who is used to being placed in uncomfortable situations would find themselves at home with this style.

Honing Your Leadership Style

Regardless of your chosen leadership style, you should hone what you are the most effective with in order to see results in the changes that you are to implement.

However, honing your skills is not just about building up on your strengths. It is also about dialing those strengths if the situation demands it while also picking up new skills along the way. You might even have to re-learn things and let go of some biases and prejudices here and there.

To Pick Up or Let Go?

When honing your leadership skill, what do you think would be the easiest? To learn new skills or to unlearn old ones? If you answer the latter, then you are correct.

The reason for this is actually simple. Learning is a purely cognitive exercise as it involves being introduced to something that is entirely new or simply enhances what you already know. For example, when managers had to learn how to use E-mail, a lot quickly noticed the system, as they understood how computers worked.

For those that did not even bother to learn the computer during the dawn of the Internet Age, they had to learn how the keyboard works first and then move on to e-mailing. Either way, it involves purely mental functions in order to improve.

Letting go, on the other hand, is an emotional experience. There is a level of discomfort at having to let go of ideas, skills, and biases that simply do not work in the current time.

For example, if you want to adopt a more democratic style of leadership, you have to face the notion of relinquishing part of your control of the organization to other people.

If you are not used to power, this might be easy. However, if you have had an uncontested grip over the company for years on end, then this task might prove to be a challenge.

Aside from this, you would have to wrestle fears of becoming irrelevant and ending up in failure when embracing change. To become a leader capable of change, then, you must learn of what to keep, pick up, and let go.

Here are five strategies that can help you do just that.

1. Getting Clear

The only way that you could possibly learn new things is if you clear about what you have to let go. This is only way to make enough "space" in your head for the new things to come in and not come in conflict with what is already there.

So, what do you want to let go of? Is it old skills you have picked up from older technologies? Is it some practices that you may learned, as you were moving through the ranks?

Whatever the case, you have to be forthcoming with what you have to get rid of. However, how should you know that something is supposed to be let go of? You can look at the performance of the organization as a whole.

More often than not, the changes in the figures can tell you if a way of thinking, practice, or technology is no longer contributing to the success of the company. If you find that such thinking is the reason why the company is not performing that well now, then you have no problems objectively replacing the old with the new.

2. Do Your Research

Ask yourself this: do you seriously think no other person has come to this dilemma other than you? More likely than not, other leaders have found themselves in this transitional period and have successfully embraced change.

As such, you have to take the time to do your research and learn from others. What did they do to make the transition? What did they have to learn, re-learn, and unlearn? How did they get others to support their vision?

You do not exactly have to follow what they did, as their circumstances may not be similar to yours. What you can do, on the other hand, is to take the bits that are applicable to your situation and build on them.

You can even ask around from your friends, mentors, and contemporaries. How do they approach change? What leadership style did they let go of or pick up in order to facilitate change? Their experiences, good or bad, will most definitely be a good source of information when implementing change in your own organization.

3. Start Small

The reason why leaders fail to change is that they take in everything at one. Of course, change is going to be daunting if you look at things from a wider perspective. However, if you look at a multi-phase, multi-year campaign as a series of challenges and steps, then everything looks a bit more manageable.

For example, you want to become less of an autocrat and more of a pacesetter. How do you get from point A to point B? This is where planning comes into play as you can set up small challenges and tasks that you can complete every day, week, or month.

Perhaps this month would include you learning how to be more diplomatic with your decision-making, the next month would involve you becoming consistent with the standards you have imposed. Every small accomplishment you take would eventually add up until you have completed the transition.

4. Balance Control and Freedom

When it comes to relinquishing control to your staff, you might find yourself becoming anxious about being put out of the loop. As a leader, you can prevent this by putting in some implementing procedures and systems that provide checks and balances with the now decentralized system of decision-making.

Being given control is not exactly easy for the recipients, either. They might find the new freedom daunting and would need someone to guide them through the process. They may even fight and bicker with each other as one person might think that his opinion is superior to everybody else's.

This is where you as the leader would come into play as you can mediate between opposing options while also consolidating ideas. After all, it is still you as the leader who is going to approve of strategies.

This way, you keep yourself in the loop with what every department is going on without micromanaging them. On the other hand, this gives your staff the morale boost that they need knowing that their contributions were ultimately valued by the higher ups.

5. **Learn from the Past**

If you take the time to look at your own history, you could get an impression as to which of your styles and practices served you well and the ones that held you back. You can even look back at the challenges you once faced and how you were able to address such.

The best part about reflection is that it gives your perspective on how you as a leader were able to handle things back. After all, past performance can be an indicator of future success. In addition, this should tell you the things that are inherent to you that could possibly serve to hinder your progress as a leader.

The point here is to never think that you are infallible as the organizational leader. You can make mistakes and have made mistakes in the past as much as you have also made the right decisions.

There are even some absurdities within yourself as a leader that you must accept and correct if you are to remain effective in the position. The less you think that you are beyond reproach, the faster it will be for you to accept change later on.

Avoiding Pitfalls

Speaking of flaws, you must also understand that leaders tend to find themselves in situations that bring out the worst of their characters. This would result in you making some leadership mistakes that would result in potentially disastrous consequences.

As such, to become a better leader, you have to know what pitfalls leaders usually put themselves and how to avoid them.

1. Thinking You Know It All

Hubris is a rather fatal quality for any leader. Assuming that you have all the answers or that what you have thought of is ultimately superior than what others can contribute can be detrimental to employee engagement. If their voices would not matter, why bother giving them a chance to speak at all?

Avoiding this problem, then, is as easy as it merely involves you never coming to the assumption that you are not an expert in everything. You must use the fact that your staff also have skills and knowledge that you do not possess to a great degree especially when implementing ideas and strategies for change.

After all, combined skills and expertise would fair outweigh individual effort.

2. Not Communicating Properly

Many leaders, even well meaning ones, do not inspire or motivate. This is not because they are intimidating or dictatorial but they just lack the ability to communicate properly.

One key element of communication is consistency and, sadly, many leaders say one thing on a meeting and another thing on a memo. This can create a lot of confusion for anyone following that person.

Another problem is this area is an inability to listen to others. For example, someone might raise an issue and you promise to do a follow-up. The only problem is that you did not. This could send the message to your staff that you were not listening or, worse, do not care at all. Thus, you lose your employees' trust, confidence, and loyalty.

The counter to this problem is Empathy. You have to convey your message in a way that it understands the needs of your employees and takes into consideration how they are going to interpret such.

Empathy is also crucial to listening as leaders are expected to put the concerns of their followers into account when making decisions. If a problem is raised, you must commit to having it solved as soon as possible.

3. Micromanagement and Constant Anger

Micromanaging is a telltale sign that you absolutely have no trust that your people can do what you ask them to do. As such, you constantly watch over them, catching on their mistakes and then stopping everything just to show them how to do it or, worse, berate them for it. Add to this one's tendency to flare up and you have one of most toxic leaders to ever have the misfortune of following.

This is what you might observe on each episode of Gordon Ramsay's show Hell's Kitchen. Every time a contestant messes up an order or is not performing to Gordon's standards, you can expect that person to receive an earful from Ramsay; right in front of everybody else. It might make for good entertainment but that constant micromanaging and hurling of insults is never, ever conducive to employee growth and development.

To avoid this, you must take the time to assess the skills and abilities of those that are following you. You have to know where your people are the strongest at individually and encourage them to develop each other. By taking a step back, you ease up a lot of pressure on the workplace, which allows people to naturally grow and develop as workers.

In addition, as for the anger, you need to work it out. Find ways to vent all that rage in more productive channels, preferably away from work. This way, you do not use your employees as targets of your wrath if ever you are on one of your bad days.

4. Underestimating the Emotional Quotient

A prevalent and often fatally potential line among leaders is "It's all Business, nothing personal".   It often means that one should leave their emotions at the door when they enter the company's doors but it is often a pretext for leaders to become abusive with their followers.

The idea that they can scream, yell, and threaten their employees and expect them to just take it all can make leaders inadvertently become the most toxic person in the workplace, reducing employee morale. In addition, a weak understanding of EQ can make leaders susceptible to losing control over their emotions during times of crisis, emotionally compromising themselves before their followers.

To avoid this, you must learn the art of not wearing your heart on your sleeves. To put it in simpler terms, you should not be the first to fly off in a rage when things do not go your way and approach problems with an objective mindset.

A leader should also be mindful of how their actions can be viewed and perceived by others and the overall morale of the workplace. By giving more praise and acknowledgement of individual efforts and group successes, a leader can instill a culture of positivity in their company, which makes the organization more open towards change.

5. Conflict Avoidance

It can be often tempting to veer away from conflict and confrontation. After all, these situations can be emotionally draining and often deals with unpleasant truths.

Whether you mean to avoid conflict or not, this behavior can make you inefficient in addressing problems in the organization. In addition, the longer a problem remains unsolved, the greater its potential effects would be to the company.

An effective leader, on the other hand, understands that conflict is inevitable. It will come in any form and will be born out of any reason. As such, they address the issue at the first instance it pops up. With this, that problem does not fester and become part of the company's culture, becoming a corporate tumor of sorts.

6. Reactionary Tendencies

A reactive leader is someone that is always caught in the moment, never planning or even anticipate for problems. This lack of thinking can cause them to lose time addressing problems that could have otherwise been prepared for while missing valuable opportunities for the company.

For instance, you might have set up a production facility but failed to even consider the fact that such equipment will have to be repaired and replaced. What happens is that you will divert funds in maintaining these facilities in the event a crucial part of the system fails.

A reactionary leader is ill prepared for crisis since such events can be seen from a mile away and, in turn, be prepared for accordingly. This also leaves a leader unable to take advantage of favorable conditions if every they arise in the market.

A proactive leader, on the other hand, plans for two or more steps ahead of everybody else and has contingency after contingency if the worst-case scenarios that they identified would occur. They also prioritize on what needs to be done and ignore other pursuits that do not help the company in reaching its ultimate goals.

7. An Ego Problem

A leader who sees their position and power as a means to inflate their self-esteem can be detrimental to the morale of the company.   If you let all that power go over your head, you run the risk of becoming an insufferable person to follow, as you are unable to see your own flaws while quick enough to point out those from other people.

The only way to deal with this situation is to balance all that power with reminding yourself of your responsibilities as a leader. You must always put the needs of others first and allow them to contribute to the effort.

Of course, making people feel appreciate and recognized work is going to help in boosting the morale of the work force. If you have an untainted view of who you are as a leader, the less your decisions will feel like a Power trip.

8. Making People Dread Being Part of the Company

Being a leader is serious business. However, that should never come at the expense of making the workplace somewhere that people could take pride in working on. In essence, you should never take the "fun" out of being affiliated with the organization.

You can do this through introducing a rewards system that gives tangible benefits for those that go beyond their call of duty while also motivating others to do better. In addition, allowing workers to "personalize" their own workspaces might look insignificant but it helps a person identify themselves to their work. Adding a bit of fun and positivity into the work goes a long way in rallying your employees especially in the middle of a transition phase.

9. Relying on Quick Fixes

No matter how difficult a problem is, you always think that there is a quick workaround for it. Quick fixes are undoubtedly available in any situation but the problem with them is longevity.

More often not, quick fixes are temporary solutions, which means that the underlying problem was never addressed.

A leader knows that quick fixes are ideal for patching leaks in the dam but, eventually, the entire structure has to be repaired. As such, they must commit to finding longer lasting solutions that employees can build on, not constantly replace in one crisis after another.

10. Not Developing People

A leader must realize that one of the most important abilities of an organization is maintaining satisfactory performance even if they are no longer around. This can be done if you develop people who can do what is necessary for the company on their own initiative.

The telltale sign of an effective leader is someone who is bold enough to fully let go of the organization they once built and can make sure that their absence does not result in a reduction in company performance and morale or, worst, utter chaos.

This is why many great leaders in various industries also were good mentors for people who would succeed them in the business or would become successful in their own ventures. For example, Thomas Alexander Scott was businesspersons who trained young men to become successful leaders themselves. One of these was Andrew Carnegie who became a renowned philanthropist who, in turn, also mentored other individuals like Charles Schwab.

In essence, a good leader thinks about making the company, not their hold over it, experience a long lifespan. This way, a company remains responsive to change and looks after the interest of everybody even if the leadership and the work force change rosters from time to time.

To Conclude

Regardless of your style as a leader, it is important to remember that you must constantly hone your leadership skills in order to become effective in your position. No leadership style out there is considered to be the best or the worst. It is all dependent on the person using such style in the hopes of bringing out the best of the people that follow them.

The point is that a good leader never shies away from change. Whether it is in enhancing their existing skill sets or letting go of what used to work, a leader must be the first to embrace change within themselves in order to facilitate the same in their organization.

In addition, it does not matter if a leader is charismatic or even that fun to be around with. Your words, actions, and intentions should be sincere enough in order to inspire others to follow you. Also, a bit of self-awareness over your own contradictions and absurdities goes a long way in solving problems, personal or organizational.

When done right, you would find that your own leadership style is always responsive to any situation, leading to breakthroughs that will take the company to newer heights.

Chapter VII: Organizational Development and Implementing Change

When implementing change in your organization, you have to ask yourself this question: to what should this change be targeted. You may answer that such changes can be for the facilities, the layout of the organizational chart, or even the policies that keep things running smoothly for now.

Those are all valid answers but they are not exactly the most correct answer. Change in an organization should always be directed towards the elements that would make such change possible in the first place, the people and the culture.

Technological changes are easy as you are only replacing aging systems with new ones. Policy changes are equally so as you are only rewording the laws that bind your company into something that is more responsive to the times.

It is changing the mindset and behaviors of the people that run the company where things are at their most challenging. It requires a paradigm shift, something that people are not the most willing to do.

So how does a leader make sure that their changes are not only effective but would last long until the next cycle? The answer lies in a strategy called Organizational Development.

What Is It?

Organizational Development is but one of many strategies wherein complete and long-lasting change can be effected on any organization. However, it stands out from the rest due to its comprehensive focus.

Where other strategies one key aspect of change in the organization, this strategy focuses on the encompassing element that makes change possible: the organization itself. It is a strategy that targets such structures such as policy making, the leadership, control and distribution of power, the delegation of tasks, and the interrelations of every position and level within the organizational chart but does so in a way that it gives every change in every sector a unified direction.

To be more detailed about this, the Organizational Development strategy would look at three key aspects of the organization.

A. The Climate

The organizational climate refers to the overall mood of the company. This is primarily dependent on the overall beliefs and attitudes of those that compose the group, the employees and the leaders.

The climate of the company can actually affect many crucial factors in the organization such as employee satisfaction, motivation, and productivity. In organizational climates, some elements may be changed during a transitional phase and this includes how the company resolves conflicts and even the way the leadership is organized.

For instance, a certain restaurant's organizational climate was very negative to the point of being toxic. Employees were no longer motivated, sales were down, and the managers were under immense pressure to earn profit.

A change in climate by making the workspace more uplifting and conducive to work might just do the trick of securing short-term goals while also helping the company achieve long-term ones. In addition, of course, all of this is achieved without sacrificing the welfare of the employees.

B. The Culture

If the climate is the mood of the company, then the culture has to do with its overall identity. Many things can form culture and this includes the norms, values, and behaviors of the employees. Even the practices and policies set in place by upper management can form part of the culture; if employees were adhering to them religiously, of course.

The organizational development strategy understands that culture must either be changed or improved on in order to implement long-lasting changes in the company.

For instance, an organization's workforce might have this strong orientation towards Family and Friendships. Perhaps they had weekly barbecues on their days off or all the staff just hang out at the same pub after a shift.

In addition, here comes the upper management who are more oriented towards Production. They might want to increase daily quotas, improve product quality, or revamp the entire production process.

At a glance, you could see that there are two cultures clashing in the same company, one that focuses on interpersonal relationships and the other on the bottom line. Those that use organizational development make it a point to have these two conflicting goals agree to a compromise. After all, both cultures have valid points and are integral to the identity of the company. All that is needed is for them to agree on some points and work on those goals.

C. The Strategies

How does a company go about attaining its goals? This is what this aspect of organization development tries to answer and thus is integral to the overall strategy.

In this aspect, the OD strategy would look at two elements: the vision and the mission. These two effectively guide the company and thus dictate whether a company is ready for change.

For example, a company vision, although not exactly worded, might paint an image of the company settling down and not expanding in its local market. This might be a good goal to achieve but it is not exactly conducive to change. As such, the vision might have to be amended.

Aside from the vision and mission statements, this part also determines if the current layout and procedures of the company is compatible with change.

Once problems in these areas are identified, the company can then go about creating strategies that will bring about the change that a leader wants for the organization. Due to its comprehensive scope, the organization development strategy can take a considerable time to be implemented.

However, if everything goes well, the changes implemented will not only be effective but would eventually be embraced as part of the new culture of the company.

Implementing Organizational Development

If this is not yet apparent to you, the organizational development strategy is to be treated as a major overhaul of the entire company. It might retain the same identity on the surface but the organization is going to be functionally different once the changes are implemented.

In addition, since this is an overhaul, the OD strategy is most often done with the coordination of consultants who can provide you with an unbiased perspective on how the changes are to be implemented. However, of course, that does not mean that you and your staff cannot do this strategy on your own.

Regardless if you seek help or not, the OD strategy will always cover the same areas, which are as follows:

1. Goal Setting

Before you can implement any change, you have to know what the result would look like for the company. There a number of goals that may be achieved under this strategy and this includes:

- Increasing overall profitability
- Improving employee morale
- Revamping company production procedures
- Increased productivity and performance
- Decreasing workplace-related accidents
- Improving workplace cohesion

Usually, departments already have identified how they can improve and only need support and oversight. This should save you a lot of time as you are now just helping your staff enact their changes as opposed to starting from the ground up.

Of course, you can also enhance these goals further and make them compatible with the company's overall strategies. In either case, it is necessary that you and other leaders take the time to sit down with each department and identify what they need in order to implement changes.

2. Restructuring

Change is often necessary when the leadership finally comes to the realization that the company cannot continue to function under its current layout. When this becomes necessary, you, other leaders, and any consultant you will hire will have to engage in a series of meetings where you will break the organizational chart and build it from the ground up.

When restructuring the organization, you might realize that new teams need to be formed while some departments and positions are redundant. As such, employees and managers might have to be reassigned and some would have to be let go of. The relationships between departments might even have to be organized to fit the new goals of the company.

This is where your ability to convey your intentions and remain transparent will become important as maintaining an open line of communication is the key to addressing dissent from the work force brought about by the restructuring.

3. Development

With the new layout for the organization comes the need to make each employee and manager correlate with each other through the chart. As such, this part of the strategy should focus on the development of two major areas of the organizational chart.

A. The Executives - In this area, the strategy would include the formation of policies and systems designed to make communication and decision making easier for managers and leaders. If a crucial decision has to be made, what are the protocols to be followed in order for that decision to be actionable?

How does one manager or supervisor in one department relay crucial information to another? In addition, how does the executive department act on problems raised by those from the lower levels?

These questions can be answered by the development of new policies that ensure a smooth flow of information across all levels.

B. The Workforce - This is perhaps the wider area to focus as it essentially covers all operations related to the business. This includes sales, marketing, production, support, and other vital technical areas of the company.

Other common areas to be covered here include technical proficiency development, communications between managers and employees, problem solving, and the creation of new products and services.

Of course, training is a matter of great importance in development. The creation of new goals and new vision would necessitate the creation of new responsibilities and systems. This, in turn, would demand that employees to be reoriented to perform under the new status quo.

Being Innovative as a Leader

Innovation might sound like a buzzword right now in business but there is no denying that it makes for a rather strong basis in one's change management strategy. In fact, it is rather synonymous to change as innovative people not only introduce and implement change; they make it a standard for the rest to follow.

People like Marie Curie, Albert Einstein, Nikola Tesla, Steve Jobs, and Elon Musk all had an eye for innovation and thus left an indelible mark in their industries. Leaders can be innovative, too, and perhaps this mindset might just be the one last push needed to make their changes all the more effective.

So, what makes a leader innovative? What qualities do they possess? Here are five tips to remember in order to become an innovative leader.

1. Become Methodical

Yes, fear can be a rather paralyzing emotion and can even stunt your growth as the organization's leader. However, fear is also grounded on some realities. Innovative ventures have led to failure in the past or were realized at great cost.

You want to push the boundaries for your business but, on the other hand, you want it to make sure you do not cause irreparable damage to it if you fail. So what is a leader supposed to do? The answer lies in taking calculated risks.

When implementing change, you should always take into consideration what could possibly happen if they were realized, both the good and bad. For instance, if you were to automate some parts of the production process, what would happen to your workers who had been doing that part of the process for years now? Would you to retrain them or let them go?

On the other hand, what happens to the quality and production rates of your facilities if some parts have become automated? Would workplace incidents also be reduced? What about maintenance and repair costs? Once you have identified all possible scenarios that can occur, you can decide whether to make some changes to your plan or create some contingencies for each scenario.

Risk Management is not about avoiding risks when making changes. It is about making sure that all your bases are covered before taking the next step forward.

2. Inspiring and Exciting

Organizational Development is always a group effort. An innovative leader then is someone who inspires his or her entire team. They are people that can convince other people to act against their instincts and perform something that they otherwise would not do.

However, being a leader is not just about telling people to do something that they are apprehensive about. It is more about opening their perspectives and inspire them to do something that they would have never thought would have been impossible.

A key element in innovation is what is called "pushing the envelope". It is the deliberate act of treading the unknown in order to tap into something that nobody else has every thought about tapping.

Steve Jobs is perhaps best known for giving his team some inspirations for Apple's next products. For example, he might just say something as if he wants all of music to be played seamlessly in one device or that he wants the screen and the keypad to be fused into one interface.

Then he just lets his team find ways to express those ideas into reality. Sure enough, the simple inspirations he gives to his team eventually became groundbreaking features found in Apple's products today, specifically the iPhone.

In as much as you would want to relinquish much of your control over the team, you can still inspire them to see things your way. This is quite effective especially if the organization is stuck in implementing change over one aspect of the company.

Perhaps your input will just provide them with the refresher they need to solve that issue to the best of their abilities.

3. Looking for (and Facing Problems)

In most cases, Innovation does not start with a "Eureka!" like idea. In most cases, it begins with a problem. Any leader is expected to address problems as soon as they pop up. However, an innovative leader does not wait for problems to become unmanageable before attempting to solve them.

Instead, these leaders are always on the lookout for issues that no one else in the organization is solving and face these challenges headfirst.

However, what you should remember in this phase is that problem solving is often a multi-phase problem. It may even involve a little of trial and error here and there until you finally crack the code.

One tip to keep in mind here is to never be beholden to your solutions. More often than not, the first solution that you would come up with is overly either complex or merely a stopgap measure. The next solutions might be a refinement of that original concept or a complete overhaul.

Whatever the case, it is important that you be relentless in looking for solutions that provide the most comprehensive answer to that problem.

The simpler and less labor intensive that solution is, the more effective it will be when solving a key problem in the company.

4. Collaboration is the Key

As was stated, implementing changes is a group effort and an innovative leader keeps this to heart. An innovative leader creates an environment where collaboration is not only possible but also easy.

For instance, you might raise an issue that nobody else has solved at that point of time. Instead of dictating what needs to be done, you can solicit the ideas of your staff. Once those ideas are laid out, you can then consolidate all of them into one strategy that would effectively solve the problem.

In essence, you are not only discovering a superior route to take when solving a problem. You are also giving your staff the chance to chart the course of the organization with their contributions. In addition, if they feel that their voices do matter in the creation of plans and policies, the more likely they are to stick by your side when times do get tough.

As Henry Ford once succinctly pointed it out, "Coming together is a beginning, keeping together is progress, and working together is Success".

5. Understanding Failure

As was previously stated a few chapters ago, Hubris is one of the most fatal qualities that any leader could possess. The notion that you cannot fail or that you are beyond reproach is something that can cripple a leader, which, in turn, seriously impedes their organization.

For instance, a plan or strategy of yours is not going well as you originally thought of. Would you allow your ego to prevail and press on despite the obvious signs of failure? Alternatively, alternatively, do you stop and get back to the drawing board?

Admitting that you fail is a bitter pill that many leaders could not swallow. In addition, if you are one of them, you have to think of it this way: perhaps the setbacks you are experiencing with your plan is just Fate telling you that you are going about the solution the wrong way.

In essence, failure to an innovative leader is just another opportunity to learn. In addition, if they take the lessons to heart, they can come up with a solution that would effectively address the issue and bring about long lasting change in the organization.

Being innovative is not just talking about good ideas. If one were to be frank about it, it is about exposing yourself to the prospect failure, which gives you the chance to hone your skills for the better.

Now that you know what it takes to implement change in the business, it is time to start applying your strategies into the organization.

Implementing Change

After all, is said and done, how does one go about making changes in the organization? Taking into consideration your vision, your leadership style, the problems you have discovered, and your organization's overall behavior towards change, there are a few steps that you have to remember to properly implement your plans into tangible changes. Here they are:

1. Find People that Your Employees Will Rally To

In most cases, the social aspect is going to have the most impact when people are faced with the notion of change. Look at this chart, for example.

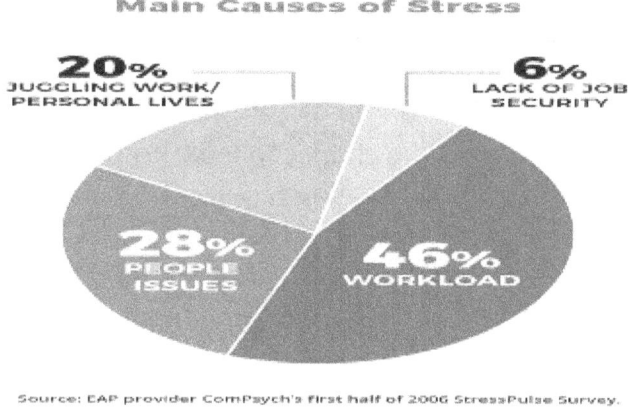

Main Causes of Stress

20% JUGGLING WORK/ PERSONAL LIVES

6% LACK OF JOB SECURITY

28% PEOPLE ISSUES

46% WORKLOAD

Source: EAP provider ComPsych's first half of 2006 StressPulse Survey.

It would show that, aside from the workload, a considerable portion of employee stress comes from fears over the security of their jobs at 6%. This can be primarily affected, in turn, by changes in the workplace.

However, a major source of stress is people-related issues at 28%. Again, this can be brought about by changes in the organizational chart as people are shuffled from one group to another depending on the needs of the company.

As such, the social aspect can determine how resistant or welcoming your staff would be towards change. So how do you make sure that such changes will be welcomed?

The answer is in Champions, which serve as your ambassadors, and liaisons that could help people accept your new vision. Think of it this way: when you, as the highest person on the organizational chart, talk about change, the people below you are a bit hesitant with your message.

They might think, "How can this corporate bigwig talk about shaking things up? He doesn't know what we go through every day!"

However, if people are promoting the same message that they know i.e. the people that they immediately work under or those that share a space with them at their work benches, then your vision of change is less abrasive to their psyches.

Your champions must work as a team in order to develop plans that would make people at their respective areas less resistant to whatever you are trying to implement. Of course, these people must be gifted with the ability to explain the benefits of the change and address the issues raised by your staff.

2. Start Small

When it comes to change, it makes sense to start with the leaders. After all, they are the ones to disseminate such information to their people, which is crucial for the entire organizational development strategy to work.

To start things off, have every leader communicate your changes and let the champions they have chosen inspire and motivate the people. It would even be better if all your leaders have already come to the consensus for change.

The reason for this is that workplace Inertia, the force that could drive any shared idea or consensus into the forefront, can determine whether such changes will be accepted or met with fierce resistance. Dissent is one such major contributor to inertia, which is why you should have any concerns addressed right at the moment that employees raised them.

Of course, change is rather hard if you do it all at once. As such, you must find one key sector in your company to apply the changes first. At a more controlled environment, you might get an impression as to how your vision is going to be accepted by everybody else in the company.

This little "experiment" will also give you the chance to expose potential flaws in your plan before widespread application. This way, you can improve areas in your overall strategy so everything will go smoothly once applied to the rest of the company.

3. Mind the Stakeholders, Too

Whether you make plans that specifically target stakeholders or simply including their concerns into the overall strategy, minding what stakeholders feel about change will also be integral to implementing long lasting change in the organization.

Keep in mind that shareholders do have a very different set of needs compared to managers and employees. Fortunately, those concerns can be broken down into a simpler need: investment security.

To elaborate, shareholders want the company to maintain a high rate of profitability even if it embraces the fluid nature of change. Apart from making sure that their investments are well protected, some shareholders also value transparency, which, again, revolves around the company's finances.

4. Pay Attention to Change at an Individual Level

Change is supposed to be widespread but every person has their own way of processing such. Individual transitions towards change may be different but fortunately, for you, they always involve three phases.

- **Letting Go:** This involves the person doing away with the standards that they have been used to.
- **Exploration:** In this phase, the person attempts to embrace change and adhere to the new standards. This is the most frustrating part as it involves trial and error as well as the development of new habits.
- **Acceptance**: Once a person has spent enough time exploring the new standards and fully letting go of the past, they can now finally embrace the change that the leadership has intended for the entire company. In essence, they have identified themselves to the new direction the company is taking and have acclimated to the new status quo.

This is the same process to follow regardless of one's position in the organizational chart. Leaders, however, have the extra concern of how to address their own discomfort towards change without negatively affecting the people that follow them. However, if they do embrace the change, they are usually the most powerful agent in that department when it comes to making other people accept the new standards.

As such, in order for this strategy to work, you have to respect the idea that people are going to lose something in the process. This could be something minimal like their own perception of comfort with the status quo or something more important like their positions and responsibilities.

In this regard, you have to be as empathetic as possible. When communicating the change, you have to be as transparent as possible so people understand the full rationale behind the change. You should also follow through with their concerns by addressing them outright or promising to tackle the issue down the road.

Lastly, you must provide for multiple opportunities towards discussing the change as not all people can get behind such at the same time. Some might need a more elaborate explanation while others simply need the assurance that their tenure in the company will not be affected.

5. Management must be Focused On

Your managers are critical to keeping the entire work force on board with the change. However, your managers can also be the most overlooked group in the entire organization when it comes to developing the skills necessary to embrace change.

Some skills that managers must possess in order to properly facilitate change include communications, interpersonal skills, team development, and coaching. These skills are necessary in the sense that they "operationalize" the desired change by making your plans actionable.

As such, you have to make sure that your managers do have this set of skills before you go about implementing the changes. They need to know what role they will exactly play in the transition period. To do this, they must provide a sufficient answer to the questions of "Why?" and "How?" of the change to be implemented. Lastly, they must have a clear idea as to what the results would look like so they can relay the same to their employees and monitor their performances properly.

6. Quell Resistance Effectively

Resistance is a naturally occurring response towards change. As such, you as a leader should anticipate for it and prepare accordingly. This might sound counterproductive, but you should allow dissent to be voiced in the planning process.

The reason for this is rather ingenious: if you allow dissent to have a voice when you are planning for change, you prevent it from appearing down the line when changes are implement. If dissent is given a voice in a meeting, then it will not appear in the production facility, in the marketing department, or in the company lounge and cafeteria.

The point is that dissent be addressed properly if you give it a platform to air its concerns at when it is still relatively small and manageable. As such, you have to encourage people to voice their concerns and assure them that it is actually okay to struggle embracing the change.

In addition, since resistance is to be expected, you have to honor the issues it raises and follow through with your promises. Perhaps the concerns raised by your people will provide opportunities for you to enhance and refine your vision for change. Ultimately, you can come up with a strategy that takes into consideration every need of every person in the company, resulting in a situation where everybody wins.

7. Maintain Communications

It is often said that dialogue is the lifeblood of change. The exchange of ideas, the raising of concerns, and the addressing of such concerns is what brings clarity in the change process.

As such, it is necessary that you continue and reinforce the dialogue all throughout the implementation of the change. This can be done through constant board and department meetings where the question "How are things going?" will be answered.

Of course, you can take advantage of your existing communication systems, especially chat rooms and forums, where employees can air out what they are feeling about the change without fear of reprisal.

8. Clarify the Metrics of Success

So what does change look like in your company? You have to clarify for everyone what the end results will be like should the changes be successfully implemented.

This way, your staff can visualize the same thing, which helps them in contributing in making that vision real. To make this possible, you must constantly communicate with your organization as to what has been achieved so far. This includes the progress of the entire company in embracing the changes.

9. Celebrate Every Milestone

As changes are embraced, your staff will eventually attain some success that you want to be replicated across the entire company. To make this possible, you have to call the attention of everyone and notify them of the successes that each department has attained in implementing changes.

Celebrating every success achieved by every team is one way of boosting morale for that team and inspiring the rest of the company to do the best that they can in implementing changes.

Of course, providing tangible and worthwhile rewards for those that do pioneer changes in their department are good motivators too.

To Conclude

Even with the best tools and strategies out there, you have to realize that implementing organizational changes is not going to be an easy affair. Change can generate fear and uncertainty as much as it inspires hope and action.

It is your skills in communicating your intended changes as well as inspiring people to do what they otherwise thought was not possible will become crucial once the implementation process starts. If you possess these skills at the very least as the organizational leader, then the transition process might just go as smoothly as possible.

Chapter VIII: Management in Times of Crisis

So far, we have talked about how to implement change in an organization. To be more specific, it is the kind of changes that you planned for or, at the very least, were prepared for.

However, what about the changes that you had no means to properly prepare your organization for since they were so sudden? Worst still, such changes can bring about monumental shifts in your company, which can be potentially disastrous.

So how can one respond to the change they never asked for? This is where a solid crisis management system comes into play. In addition, in order to come up with one for your organization, there are a few things that you have to understand first.

What is a Crisis?

An organizational crisis is any event that is specific, unexpected, and far off the routine operations that can create a high level of certainty within the group. It can even pose a threat to the organization's ability to achieve its goals or, worse, can seriously affect its very existence and bottom line.

To be more specific, a crisis is anything that could:

A. Threaten a business's product line or a business unit.
B. Damage the financial performance and security of a company.
C. Put the company in a situation where it can potentially harm the health and wellbeing of its community.
D. Utterly or partially destroy the public's trust in the company and forever change its image towards investors.

History itself has plenty of examples on how a crisis changed a company forever. Prior to that disastrous oil spill in Alaska on March 24, 1989, the Exxon Company had a rather strong reputation as an oil distributor.

Now, the company might continue to exist but it also has to deal with lawsuits, public backlash, and the infamous reputation of irreparably damaging a considerable expanse of land and sea as well as the economy of several Alaskan towns.

Crisis also struck Malaysia Airlines when two of its international flights ended in tragedy when two of its planes plunged in oceans, leaving hundreds of passengers and crewmembers dead.

It also did not help matters that they had a slow response to the situations, leaving their reputation today considerably soiled.

The Nature of Crisis

More often than not, crisis is unexpected by design. This is mostly due to man's own cognitive limits. In essence, you cannot exactly see the future and your organization can only do so much in attending to one priority, threat, or concern at a time.

However, there are also instances when crises can be averted. Some situations like the Financial Crisis of the late 2000s did not exactly occur overnight. Instead, it was a series of minor occurrences that contributed and resulted in a massive and downwards shift in the economy.

To put it in other words, there are some forms of crisis that telegraph not exactly when they are going to happen but that they are going to happen soon. As a result, how much of such a crisis impedes an organization's performance is utterly dependent on how their preparations.

However, even with every chance to prepare, there is also the psychological factor amongst leaders and industry figures. Some, due to being comfortable with their organization's current status quo, might deny the eventuality of an upcoming crisis. As such, they are unable to prepare properly or respond to the event as it occurs.

Another disturbing trend seen recently is that crises have increased in their lethality towards company especially in recent years. Social media, for example, allows consumers to constantly monitor companies for wrongdoings. In the event that a company does not fall in line with public consensus, they can definitely face a public relations problem in the online world.

In addition, it is not just the internet that increases the effects of crisis for companies. The changing stability of the environment urges companies to be more ecologically conscious. Those that fail to change their policies to be more eco-friendly are seen as corporate pariahs whose products and services do not instill loyalty amongst the consuming public.

In addition, speaking of consumers, the average person right now is more discerning in their purchases. If they see that a company does not have their best interest, they will thwart any advance that company does no matter how good the marketing to push it is.

Overall, Crisis has a way of completely changing a company as well as its standing in the community or industry it operates in. As such, the ability to meet crisis head on and cope with the worst effects that it could bring is a vital skill for any leader.

Effective Crisis Management

Unlike the more neutral forms of change, Crisis was always designed to negatively affect a company. In addition, it can strike at any moment, announced or otherwise.

This is why you as a leader should come to terms with the fact that a crisis can pop up at any second and it is your duty to prepare the company for such occurrences. When planning for a crisis, there are several steps that you have to remember:

1. Make a Plan

Your plan is a key element in addressing a crisis before it happens or mitigate its effects when it does occur. In addition, with every plan, it begins with a set of objectives.

For crisis management plans, the objectives may include the following:

- Protect employees and leaders from the fallout.
- Protect the bottom line.
- Maintain the company's public image or salvage whatever is left of it, depending on the damage, that crisis has inflicted on the organization's reputation.
- Mitigate dissent and outrage from the public.
- Restore the company's orientation towards its original mission and vision.

There are also other worthwhile objects to follow including maintaining an open line of communication with the public. The point is that the strategy here revolves around ensuring the company's survival in one form or another.

2. Elect an Ambassador/Spokesperson

Any event that could affect the public and its interest will undoubtedly attract the attention of the media. As such, it is highly important that your company can speak your stance as consistently as possible. This means delivering the same message with the same tenor and usage of terminologies.

Instead of having multiple people do all the taking for your organization, you must select only one person to do all of that. The presence of a spokesperson can be beneficial in two ways. First, it limits confusion and miscommunication as a singular messenger is better at consistency than multiple ones.

Second, it gives the media a go-to person for the company, establishing a connection of sorts. So, instead of haranguing your employees (and you), media people can now focus their attention to one person who is going to speak in behalf of the company. This could relieve a lot of pressure from the company so it can focus on dealing with the crisis.

3. Honesty Is The Key

In addition, since the media is now at your doorstep, you have to be more careful with what the organization is going to say to the public. In addition, nothing can attract media frenzy more than an insincere message. This is what happened with Malaysia Airlines when their public apology was perceived to be insincere, causing further divide between the company and the public.

You also have to remember that you cannot fully control public opinion over your company. If it makes a mistake, you can be certain that rumors and negative comments from the public will start generating.

Your only defense to this is in maintaining an open and honest line of communication with the public. Have the organization project an image of transparency through all available media such as news and interviews. If done right, you can diffuse a large amount of tension between the company and the public.

4. Inform Employees, Too

Aside from the public, your work force must also be informed of the steps you are taking to address the situation. Do remember that the loyalty of your employees towards the organization is only secured if you do not keep them in the dark.

Try to maintain an open line of communication with them and address any issues that might arise from them. Remember, your employees also have their internal rumor mill. If they lose faith in the company itself, you may have a hard time raising their morale as the worst effects occur in the crisis.

5. Deal With Customers and Suppliers

If possible, never let your customers and suppliers learn of your crisis from the media. They should hear it from you first so they do not impulsively call of their transactions with you without hearing from you first.

However, communicating with them about the crisis is not enough. You also have to inform them of the steps you are taking to solve the problem and that they will be updated of any progress done.

6. Over Communicate

When it comes to communications while dealing with a crisis, Overkill is always acceptable. Take every opportunity to communicate what has been done to the media, to your employees, to your shareholders, and your customers and suppliers. This gives the impression that your company is on top of things which gives the assurance that it might just survive this ordeal.

Also, this deals with the fact that the news right now operates on a 24/7 cycle. If your crisis management system operates on the same standard, then your company might just be successful in retaining working relationships with various sectors in the public.

7. Take Advantage of Social Media

As of now, social media is the most active channel of information and news. In addition, your reputation as an organization can be enhanced, formed, or destroyed by how Netizens treat the information they receive about your company and its crisis.

If possible, set up a social media team within your company whose purpose is to give your company a strong online presence in channels like Facebook, Twitter, and Instagram. They must maintain constant activity there, addressing legitimate issues and questions being raised while assuring the public that the situation is being handled to the best of the company's abilities.

Letting Go

When worst comes to worst, such as in a financial crisis, the best strategy for survival is often to downsize your operations. If resources are low, and goodwill in the public has all been exhausted, there is a certain risk to be entailed from insisting on operating on the same scope or maintaining the same size of a work force. There are things that you have to let go of in order to stay afloat.

This is perhaps one of the hardest decisions you will have to make but, if the organization is to survive, some sacrifices have to be made. If you ever the business in a precarious situation, there are a few tips that you have to keep in mind.

A. Make a List

This part is basic but is essential to your survival. Make a list of all the sectors and channels that your company is operating, the strategies that you are using, and the tools at your disposal. Then, you and your staff should ask this question: is this part of the company still integral to achieving its visions based on its performance?

To answer that question, you must arrange all assets according to their performance with the top performers at the top and the least-performing ones at the bottom. Also, make sure that you have all the relevant data you have on these departments and assets such as their monthly performance, financial records, and other metrics that could help in your decision.

B. Remain as Objective as Possible

Regardless of how big your company is, cleaning house is always hard. After all, you may have to let go of pet projects and ventures that you and your organization have spent a lot of time and care developing.

When you have to confront the fact that something (or someone) is to be let go, you have to maintain an objective mindset as you address issues. For letting go of departments and people, you have to be as honest with them but do so in a way that does not cause panic or reduce workplace morale. Always make it a point that your decision was based on their performance, not their character.

However, of course, never leave the door closed for these people to return if things take a turn for the better.

C. Take a Hit

Lastly, you must give the impression that such downsizing is also affecting you as an individual. More often than not, the crisis is going to change the layout of the entire organization provided, of course, that the company is going to survive this ordeal.

For example, if you have to let go of people and departments, it would be prudent if you and other leaders take a pay cut too until things turn out for the better. Crises, after all, are hard experiences to go through so a bit of solidarity with the rest of the company is going to help in maintaining morale and keeping everyone focused on addressing the problem.

D. Setting Up a Succession Plan

In some cases, it is you yourself that has to let go of the company by stepping down. Some worst-case scenarios could cause the entire organization, from employees to stockholders, to lose faith in your leadership.

Now, a loss of faith might be inconceivable but it often happens; even with the best leaders out there. Perhaps your efforts in addressing the situation and that somebody else is better fit to pull the company out of this mess.

Alternatively, the shareholders and managers might have come to the decision to sell the company to another who might be more capable of leading it out of this situation. Either way, any fiduciary relationship you have with the organization is about to expire.

In as much as you vacating your position immediately is ideal at this situation, it would be better that you set up some systems that would make a smooth transition between leaders.

Who is going to succeed you? What qualities should that person possess? How are they going to be placed in power? Such concerns need to be addressed before or during times of crisis so that the company does not remain leaderless for too long.

When implementing changes in your organization, it is important that you and the rest of the management should come up with a comprehensive success plan. This should detail when and how leaders can be replaced due to various situations and who would act as its interim managers while executive positions are vacant.

To Sum Things Up

Remember that a mismanaged crisis has the potential to destroy in seconds whatever reputation your organization has been building up for years or decades. Alternatively, a good management system can keep vital sectors of the company and the public informed that measures have been taken to diffuse the situation.

There is also no harm in seeking advice from experts on how to handle a crisis as it occurs. You may even admit that you or your company may not have what it takes to fully deal with things right now. If you are honest with how things are going, you might just get the help that you need to pull the organization out of this fiasco.

Chapter IX: Self-Discipline

How to Acquire Self-Discipline

What is Self-discipline?

Self-discipline refers to the code of conduct that one prescribes to carry out a particular activity in the microcosm or to establish and implement a specific behavior pattern under all circumstances. For example, it is task-oriented self-discipline if you want to lose 10 pounds and decide on a three-month routine to follow a specific scheme. On the other hand, if you agree to abide by the Golden Rule "To do as you would to others," then you will discipline yourself so that you can obey a consistent pattern of behavior in your relationships.

Self-discipline is a code of conduct that one prescribes for itself and pursues a specific goal under all circumstances.

Create an Intention

Is described as an intense passion for a strong purpose, together with a definite action to achieve the desired result. The development of a statement is an expression of intent. In our case, the goal is to lose 10 pounds in 3 months. The passion comes from visualizing myself that my target has already been accomplished with all good feelings and positive things that come with achievement. Once formed in the consciousness, it will look like this, "On 12 April 2009, you weight 130 livres of my current 140 livres, so I can lead a rich and healthy life and look slim and sexy." To have auto-discipline, link first -a connection between the various components that lead to the final result. To lose weight—connecting means to link the dietary components, nutrition, exercise, immediate fulfillment, desire, disciplinary pain, and pleasure in achieving the result. When connecting the various elements, you can decide what components help us and what components hinder us from maintaining a specific bodyweight in your self-discipline. The list thus created must be prioritized and tasks assigned to each element to work on. The elements must always be balanced in order to achieve our goal.

Create a plan

A plan consists of daily increments, which will lead to the result. The first part of the plan is to start where you are. Exercise is an aspect that you have to focus on to lose the desired weight. Your workout routine, however, will depend on your current physical condition. If you have never exercised and the training plan begins with an intense 1 hour per day in the gym, the physical body can break down in a short time. You need to evaluate your physical condition every three months, identify the required physical condition, and develop a plan for gradual, incremental conditioning of your body to the desired state. A schedule must include something to do every day, which scales the day before.

Each plan is unique to itself

Although it is not hard to build a plan for yourself, you must draw up the right plan for your full commitment. If a program is contraindicative or difficult to follow, it causes the plan to be abandoned. Therefore, the strategy sometimes has to be adjusted to what is possible and then slowly adapted to the ultimate goal. Often, our ego or ignorance comes in the way of change. It is then necessary for us to have a coach, mentor, facilitator, trainer, or teacher, depending on what you do.

Create a Practice

Develop a process without adding itself to the objectives. Objectives are temporary, and therefore any attachment to the objectives leads to a sense of finitude once the aim is achieved. After the affirmation is made, the objective is achieved, so there is no reason to attach itself to the objective. An independent activity leads to self-discipline as a personality characteristic that can be repeated to accomplish specific objectives. As beings looking for pleasure and pain avoidance, you always pursue goals consciously and unconsciously. There is, therefore, no start or finish of work. The most important part of self-discipline is work.

Practice needs the qualities of constant and enduring dedication, devotion, enthusiasm, and dedication. Once these qualities are established, the practice itself becomes independent, steady, and stable. As they become stronger and a habit, what is practiced becomes a practitioner's natural way of living. The acts and movement to the end are effortless and self-perpetuating and self-supporting.

If practice becomes a habit over a long period of time, when one pays full attention to one another through enthusiasm and constant devotion and attention, the effect becomes a natural result spontaneously from within. The everyday battle of strength, energy, and other emotional crutches depends on will. A biofeedback loop-much like a drug-is then created, in which you move and achieve your goals naturally and effortlessly.
Celebrate
Celebrating is an act of celebration and gratitude. This leads to the integration of the experience. Those who forget to celebrate often describe the experience as painful and find it harder and harder to achieve their goals. No happiness, passion, and enjoyment only the memories remain of the hard work and pain-what you sometimes call "lack of motivation" or "burn out."

The celebration can be a significant gesture or anything that brings joy. It is also possible to share positive feelings with friends, colleagues, and loved ones. Recording accomplishments and writing letters of gratitude to one's self is a way for many positive people to document their achievements so that they can at any time catch the good feelings by looking at these articles.

A Daily Self-Discipline Plan:
Wake up time
Wake up activity
Physical exercise, Breathing exercise and Meditation
Reflection, Appreciation and Affirmation
Create an Intention of the day
Daily activity includes at least one activity towards goal and purpose
Family time and time for loved ones
Reading
Playtime
Journal your day
Attitude of Gratitude

Practicing such a routine every day leads us to self-discipline, which binds us to our origins and leads the people around us and us to happiness. You have to learn to understand it.

Self-discipline in the work-place

Leaders are generally required to play responsibilities. These responsibilities can include managing other persons, delegating work, resolving problems or resolving conflicts, and working on their tasks and objectives. Despite competing priorities, a leader finds it difficult to focus his attention on a particular task unbroken. Self-discipline is the ability to withstand desires, concentrate, and see the completion of tasks. It is characterized by determination, the willingness of a leader to devote his attention to a mission until it is completed. Leaders who are self-disciplinary are not distracted easily. Despite specific goals or requirements, they may sustain focus.

Self-discipline at work helps leaders to pay full attention to the job. Evidence has shown that leaders with a good sense of self-control and commitment are more likely to work diligently1 and2. Furthermore, setting aside time for specific tasks shows two things directly. Firstly, it shows the type of activities or initiatives that their members prioritize. Firstly, it shows that their members are willing and able to sleep and contribute to their job. Self-discipline is not only an effective tool for leaders who want to do more success every day; it can inspire workers to follow the leader's example.

As you assess your level of self-discipline, ask yourself:

Am I set expectations for what I want to do each day?

Do I have broken all day long?

Have I taken measures to limit my distractions and temptations?

Do I have a reasonable time to complete the tasks?

Should I delegate research and decision-making efficiently where possible?

Was I aware of my daily work routine?

Note the motivation rules:

There are some suggestions from the literature on motivation and objectives that can help you improve consistency in your work.

Next, set your targets where possible. They should be large enough to create a sense of achievement, but small enough to be realistic and feasible. Breaking a broad goal into smaller, more achievable components will help maintain your motivation over time.

If you have a personally meaningful and motivating target, it is easier to focus your efforts on achieving this goal. If you make a goal, large and small, you will take the time to reward your efforts. The process of setting realistic goals and working towards these goals and celebrating your successes will maintain your motivation and engagement in your tasks and enable you to remain focused and concentrated over time.

Often take breaks: self-discipline is like a muscle. Through practice, you will develop and strengthen your ability. But you can also get tired and find your power drained. The more you use your control in one day, the more this resource is diminished4.

Fortunately, taking a break from your work, as with our muscles, is a simple strategy to regain this lost discipline and focus. Regular breaks should be scheduled, time to leave your desks or computers. Furthermore, leaders should plan breaks that are appropriate for their daily work. For example, if you find that specific tasks leave you exhausted or fatigued, consider preparing this task at a time when you can replace it immediately with a long break or work requiring little active self-control. Try to track how you feel about your jobs. This will encourage you to schedule your time more efficiently to get the most out of your day and self-control.

Recall, the type of tasks a leader finds particularly tricky or stressful vary between individuals. Your work schedule and subsequent breaks should be personalized according to your interests.

Eliminate temptations and distractions: self-discipline is better strengthened with daily practice, like many skills. It is a learned behavior that you can teach yourself more often, not an inherent ability. One of the best ways to excel is to remove the items that distract you from your job. This can look different for people. Many people may want to shut the door to their office to help preserve their focus. For others, it is better to keep emails private, switch cell phones off, or block tenting websites.

So, start removing obstacles, go around the day as you usually would. Whenever your work is taken care of, note what distracted you. Over a few days, patterns or distractions categories will emerge. Identifying these lets, you decide how they can be prevented. Note, it takes time to change the way you work, so be careful as you remove distractions from your workday. Competitive priorities and urgent tasks are often a reality for leaders, and distractions are sometimes inevitable. Self-discipline allows you to stay focused on non-essential interruptions.

Now begin to increase self-discipline. The following steps will help you improve self-control in the workplace: Make your time to decide. Decision-making is one of the tasks often exclusively carried out by leaders. These include deciding how to allocate resources, focusing on your unit's goals, and assigning work to each employee. Evidence has shown that decision-making is a stressful activity, and it is hard for leaders to retain self-control and concentration following crucial decisions5. Treat decision-making as any other task: allow yourself enough time to make the right choice and recover from all the stress caused by this job. When you make important decisions when juggling other goals, you will only be distracted and lead to low self-control.

Remove load. Reduce load. While leaders can often make decision-making, delegation is an essential tool to prevent you from overcharging yourself. When appropriate, encourage the employees to make decisions, either by collecting more knowledge or by offering their opinions and know-how. This not only decreases a leader's commitment but also indicates literature that engagement in some decision-making will boost employees ' long-term self-discipline and motivation 5. Delegating some of the work you and your colleagues do in decision making can be mutually beneficial.

Practice diligent meditation. Meditation of mindfulness is becoming popular in the world of work and is often offered as a solution to a variety of organizational problems. Yet good consciousness training helps you develop your concentration by learning to concentrate on a particular point, like your respiration while letting feelings or thoughts go by without influencing you. Regular meditation can have several positive effects for leaders, but individual awareness practice decreases impulsiveness in self-discipline and allows you to maintain concentration and control over the whole day. SIGMA provides a free, controlled mediation course for eight weeks that can help you grow your skills and thus strengthen your self-discipline in your work.

To Conclude: Self-discipline

Self-discipline is one of the main and most useful skills that all should have. This ability is essential in every area of life, and while most people recognize its value, very few do anything to enhance it.

Contrary to common belief, self-discipline is not hard for you or a restricted lifestyle. Self-discipline means: self-control, which is a sign of inner power and self-control, actions, and reactions.

Self-discipline gives you the power to obey and execute your decisions, without changing your mind, and is thus an essential condition for achieving your goals.

With this skill, you will persevere with your decisions and plans until you do so. It is also an inner strength that helps you overcome addictions, delays, and laziness and to go on with anything you do.

Final Conclusion

After everything has been said and done, there is still one thing that you should ask yourself:

What has been achieved with Change?

Managing change in an organization is a complex process. After all, it involves different sectors of a company as well as the people that make up such groups. Evaluating whether or not your changes were successful is something that involves more than reading reports and checking off objectives in your list. However, this is essential in determining how successful your changes were and what needs to be done next.

Therefore, the challenge now is to measure something as complicated as organizational change? To do so, there are four variables that you should take into consideration.

Variable #1: What was changed?

The first thing that you should address is the impact of the choices that you and your staff made into the organization itself. This involves taking a good look at your change system and determining whether it was a "perfect fit" for the company.

Here are some questions that you have to answer to determine the impact made by your changes.

- Was your change strategy in line with your overall business strategy?
- Did the change fit with the organization's culture?
- Are the choices that you have made helping the business in the marketplace?

For instance, let us say that your change involved establishing a culture of transparency and innovation in the workplace. To see if such changes were effective, you would have to compare and contrast the strategies that you are using and how they fit with the new direction for the company.

In addition, you should look if such culture actually produced something tangible that helped the market improve its standing in the marketplace.

Variable #2: How much of your Changes were implemented?

More often than not, many changes planned by an organization stay just that: plans. All of them were left in paper as those that were responsible for implementing them failed to follow through.

Measuring if your vision was completely implemented can be done through tracking metrics within your organization. Supposed that your change involves the acquisition of newer equipment and systems. Were there any new equipment purchased and installed in the departments? In addition, if so, was there a comprehensive orientation and training process to help the workers get the hang out of using the new equipment?

What you should be looking for in this aspect if the plans that your organization has been translated into tangible action, not just merely actionable.

Variable #3: Was there a Change in Organizational Behavior?

Assuming that the letter, the next question you should ask, properly executed the changes is if the changes implemented resulted in changes in how people think and behave in the organization. Be careful, though, as this metric is not as easy to measure as you would think.

If you were attempting to introduce a culture of innovation, are your employees more innovative now? If you introduced a culture of transparency, are your employees being more honest with each other now. Alternatively, if you introduced a culture of collaboration and friendly competition, has infighting been reduced in the workplace?

This is not something that you would see in a chart or a report. Instead, you have to look at how people move and treat each other whenever they are doing their work for the company.

If there are no observable changes in employee behavior, then the cultural changes are mostly surface-level. This is an indicator that you have to push for changes that are more comprehensive in the next cycle.

Variable #4: What has the organization achieved?

So, assuming that your vision was properly translated into actionable strategies, that your strategies were fully implemented, and the overall company culture was changed, the last thing to tackle is this: did all of those changes ultimately help the company with its bottom line?

Change should ultimately lead to tangible and beneficial results for the company. This includes an increase in customer satisfaction, improvements in workplace productivity, a boost in company morale, and, of course, increases in sales figures.

These results are a telltale sign that what you were implementing is not only accepted by your people but has been expressed into products that the rest of the market could appreciate. The better your brand's performance is in the market, the more apparent the changes that you were implementing are.

In addition, if the changes that you are bringing did not translate to good figures, your evaluation would still tell you what to work on for the next change cycle.

Thank you for taking the time to read this book. As of this point, it is expected that you know the basics of implementing change within your organization and how to make the effects it brings last for as long as possible. Now, all that is left to do is to create your vision and translate all that you have learned here into actionable strategies.

Felicity Gray